Marcelo Serrano Zanetti

**Software Engineering**

Marcelo Serrano Zanetti

# Software Engineering

## A Complex Systems Approach

Südwestdeutscher Verlag für Hochschulschriften

**Impressum / Imprint**
Bibliografische Information der Deutschen Nationalbibliothek: Die Deutsche Nationalbibliothek verzeichnet diese Publikation in der Deutschen Nationalbibliografie; detaillierte bibliografische Daten sind im Internet über http://dnb.d-nb.de abrufbar.
Alle in diesem Buch genannten Marken und Produktnamen unterliegen warenzeichen-, marken- oder patentrechtlichem Schutz bzw. sind Warenzeichen oder eingetragene Warenzeichen der jeweiligen Inhaber. Die Wiedergabe von Marken, Produktnamen, Gebrauchsnamen, Handelsnamen, Warenbezeichnungen u.s.w. in diesem Werk berechtigt auch ohne besondere Kennzeichnung nicht zu der Annahme, dass solche Namen im Sinne der Warenzeichen- und Markenschutzgesetzgebung als frei zu betrachten wären und daher von jedermann benutzt werden dürften.

Bibliographic information published by the Deutsche Nationalbibliothek: The Deutsche Nationalbibliothek lists this publication in the Deutsche Nationalbibliografie; detailed bibliographic data are available in the Internet at http://dnb.d-nb.de.
Any brand names and product names mentioned in this book are subject to trademark, brand or patent protection and are trademarks or registered trademarks of their respective holders. The use of brand names, product names, common names, trade names, product descriptions etc. even without a particular marking in this works is in no way to be construed to mean that such names may be regarded as unrestricted in respect of trademark and brand protection legislation and could thus be used by anyone.

Coverbild / Cover image: www.ingimage.com

Verlag / Publisher:
Südwestdeutscher Verlag für Hochschulschriften
ist ein Imprint der / is a trademark of
OmniScriptum GmbH & Co. KG
Heinrich-Böcking-Str. 6-8, 66121 Saarbrücken, Deutschland / Germany
Email: info@svh-verlag.de

Herstellung: siehe letzte Seite /
Printed at: see last page
**ISBN: 978-3-8381-3884-8**

Zugl. / Approved by: Zürich, ETH Zürich, Diss. ETH Nr. 21653, 2013

Copyright © 2014 OmniScriptum GmbH & Co. KG
Alle Rechte vorbehalten. / All rights reserved. Saarbrücken 2014

# Preface

This book is based on the doctoral thesis I wrote in Switzerland, while studying complex systems and software engineering at ETH Zürich [238]. We focus on the complexity of software engineering, which requires an interdisciplinary approach. Moreover, a complex approach, due to the fact that software engineering is influenced by the interaction of a large number of different aspects, of technical and also of social nature. Here, the potential impact of complexity on software engineering practice and research is illustrated by studies focused on the dynamics of the social organization and the software architecture of open source software projects. The results presented in this book will increase in relevance and scope as the software industry moves forward towards global software engineering, which is embracing many of the practices put forward by the open source model for software development. Finally, while the results focus on software engineering issues, the methodology presented here is of broader interest, and can be useful in different domains. For example, the quantification of properties of network topologies associated with machine learning methods is a powerful approach, and can be applied to other kinds of social data.

São Luís,  *Marcelo S. Zanetti*
July 2014

# Acknowledgment

I would like to thank my supervisor and referee *Prof. Dr. Dr. Frank Schweitzer* for the opportunity of having me as one of his students, for supporting me in moments of great confusion and also for patiently replying my annual question on the subject of whether I was going to be "fired" in the next round. Special thanks also go to my co-referee *Prof. Dr. Giuseppe Valetto* for agreeing to review this doctoral thesis under the tight schedule imposed by a higher order power, and for his insightful feedback with respect to my research. Not to forget *Prof. Dr. Juliana Sutanto*, for kindly agreeing and finding the time to preside my doctoral defense, and the combined efforts of all of my co-authors *Claudio, David, Emre, Frank* and *Ingo*. Especially *Claudio* and *Ingo*, the ones I annoyed the most. For all the people I met at the Chair of Systems Design: aren't we all just passing through? As my sergent once said, "wise is he who learns from all", thus my thanks to all of the current members *Adiya, Antonios, Claudio, David, Emre, Frank, Georgi, Ingo, Ivana, Kári, Mario, Nicolas P., Nicolas W., Pavlin, Rahel, Rebekka, René, Vahan, Victor* and all the others that left us before. Finally, I can not forget Assiya for all her love and support during my studies *** :P tonguelinha ***.

Aos meus pais
José Américo e Marilene

# Contents

| | |
|---|---:|
| Contents | 9 |
| Abstract | 13 |
| Summary | 15 |
| **1 Introduction** | **17** |
| 1.1 Complex, Not Simply Complicated | 17 |
| 1.2 Software Engineering and Complexity | 20 |
| 1.3 Focus of the Thesis | 23 |
|     1.3.1 Contributions: Part I - Collaborative Bug Handling | 28 |
|     1.3.2 Contributions: Part II - Software Modularity | 30 |
| **I Collaborative Bug Handling** | **31** |
| **2 Quantifying Social Organization** | **33** |
| 2.1 Introduction | 34 |
| 2.2 Social Organization: A Network Perspective | 35 |
|     2.2.1 Building Social Networks from Bug Reports | 35 |
|     2.2.2 Network Measures | 37 |
| 2.3 Comparative Analysis of OSS Communities | 38 |
| 2.4 Threats to Validity | 42 |
| 2.5 Conclusion | 42 |

| | | | |
|---|---|---|---|
| **3** | **A Case Study on Centralization** | | **44** |
| | 3.1 | Introduction | 45 |
| | 3.2 | Collaborative Structures in Software Engineering | 46 |
| | 3.3 | Methodology | 47 |
| | | 3.3.1 Data Collection | 48 |
| | | 3.3.2 Network Construction | 49 |
| | | 3.3.3 Network Measures | 51 |
| | | 3.3.4 Interviews with prominent contributors | 53 |
| | 3.4 | Dynamics of Social Organization and Performance | 53 |
| | | 3.4.1 Community Cohesion | 54 |
| | | 3.4.2 Centralization | 58 |
| | | 3.4.3 Bug Handling Performance | 59 |
| | | 3.4.4 Discussion | 61 |
| | 3.5 | Threats to Validity | 63 |
| | 3.6 | Conclusion | 64 |
| **4** | **Emotions and Contributors Activity** | | **66** |
| | 4.1 | Introduction | 67 |
| | 4.2 | Related Work | 68 |
| | | 4.2.1 Social Dynamics of Open Source Software | 68 |
| | | 4.2.2 Emotions in Social Media | 69 |
| | | 4.2.3 Social Resilience and Contributor Motivation | 70 |
| | 4.3 | GENTOO Datasets | 70 |
| | | 4.3.1 Bug reports | 70 |
| | | 4.3.2 Developer mailing list | 71 |
| | | 4.3.3 Sentiment analysis | 71 |
| | 4.4 | The departure of a central contributor | 72 |
| | | 4.4.1 Effect on performance | 73 |
| | | 4.4.2 Changes in collective emotions | 73 |

|       |       |                                              |     |
|-------|-------|----------------------------------------------|-----|
| 4.5   |       | Emotions and inactivity                      | 77  |
|       | 4.5.1 | Activity modes                               | 78  |
|       | 4.5.2 | Contributor emotions                         | 79  |
|       | 4.5.3 | Activity tendencies                          | 80  |
|       | 4.5.4 | Real-time prediction                         | 82  |
| 4.6   |       | Threats to Validity                          | 84  |
| 4.7   |       | Conclusion                                   | 84  |

## 5 Triaging Bugs with Social Networks — 86

|       |       |                                              |     |
|-------|-------|----------------------------------------------|-----|
| 5.1   |       | Introduction                                 | 87  |
| 5.2   |       | Social Aspects in Bug Report Processing      | 88  |
| 5.3   |       | Study Design and Methodology                 | 90  |
|       | 5.3.1 | Data Retrieval                               | 91  |
|       | 5.3.2 | Network Construction                         | 93  |
|       | 5.3.3 | Network Measures                             | 94  |
| 5.4   |       | User Centrality and Bug Report Quality       | 95  |
|       | 5.4.1 | Analysis                                     | 99  |
| 5.5   |       | Classification of Bugs with Social Networks  | 101 |
| 5.6   |       | Threats to Validity                          | 104 |
| 5.7   |       | Conclusion                                   | 106 |

# II Software Modularity — 109

## 6 Monitoring Software Modularity — 111

|       |                     |     |
|-------|---------------------|-----|
| 6.1   | Introduction        | 112 |
| 6.2   | Methodology         | 113 |
| 6.3   | Results             | 116 |
| 6.4   | Related Work        | 120 |
| 6.5   | Threats to Validity | 122 |

|       |       |                                                          |     |
|-------|-------|----------------------------------------------------------|-----|
| 6.6   |       | Conclusion                                               | 123 |

## 7 Improving Software Modularity          125

|       |       |                                                          |     |
|-------|-------|----------------------------------------------------------|-----|
| 7.1   |       | Introduction                                             | 126 |
| 7.2   |       | Methods                                                  | 127 |
|       | 7.2.1 | Datasets                                                 | 127 |
|       | 7.2.2 | Software Dependency Networks                             | 128 |
|       | 7.2.3 | A Complex Systems Approach to ReModularization           | 128 |
|       | 7.2.4 | An Alternative Metric for Coupling and Cohesion          | 135 |
|       | 7.2.5 | SOMOMOTO: An Eclipse Plugin for ReModularization         | 136 |
| 7.3   |       | Results                                                  | 136 |
|       | 7.3.1 | The Temperature and the Equilibrium Configuration        | 136 |
|       | 7.3.2 | Remodularization Performance of our Strategy             | 141 |
|       | 7.3.3 | Move Refactoring in Empirical Data                       | 141 |
|       | 7.3.4 | SOMOMOTO in Action                                       | 142 |
| 7.4   |       | Threats to Validity                                      | 143 |
| 7.5   |       | Related Work                                             | 145 |
| 7.6   |       | Conclusion                                               | 146 |

## 8 Conclusions          149

|       |       |                                                          |     |
|-------|-------|----------------------------------------------------------|-----|
| 8.1   |       | Summary                                                  | 149 |
| 8.2   |       | Scientific Scope                                         | 151 |
|       | 8.2.1 | Social Organization & Management                         | 152 |
|       | 8.2.2 | Computer Science                                         | 153 |
|       | 8.2.3 | Physics of Complex Networks                              | 154 |
| 8.3   |       | Outlook and Concluding Thoughts                          | 155 |

## Bibliography          157

# Abstract

This thesis addresses the complexity of software engineering. We first define what we mean by *complexity*. Then, we proceed by discussing a number of examples of software engineering processes strongly tied to complexity, both of social and technical nature. We specifically focus on two of these processes: *collaborative bug handling* and *software modularity*. The former is the result of social interactions, taking place within open source software communities, while processing and resolving software *bugs*. The latter determines how software architectures should be structured in order to foster their maintainability. This thesis is divided into two parts: one studying the role and dynamics of social interactions, while the other focuses on the growth of source code and how software dependencies are organized. We argue that social interactions and software dependencies share a topological structure that can be addressed quantitatively by the application of *complex networks theory*. We provide a number of examples illustrating how useful this framework can be. We show that we can measure possible threats against community resilience when discussing a case study on centralization. Furthermore, we use social network analysis to create a social information filtering scheme with a remarkable high accuracy, when applied to predict which bug reports can be fixed. We also discuss how the deterioration of modularity can impact on project management costs, and we propose an efficient method to restore software modularity, by automatically reorganizing source code. We argue that the results presented via these two perspectives, namely social interactions and software dependencies, can be unified in software engineering under the *socio-technical congruence* framework. We emphasize that our results have an impact far beyond the realm of software engineering. Specifically, we argue that our findings are of broader interest to the social sciences, contributing to the fast growing field of *computational social sciences*.

# Summary

## Chapter 1: Introduction

We start with a short review on complexity, and briefly highlight the complexity of a number of software engineering processes. We present our methodology and contributions.

## Part I: Collaborative Bug Handling

Part I covers chapters 2–5, and discusses the quantification of social organization in open source bug handling communities.

### Chapter 2: Quantifying Social Organization

We present a quantitative methodology based on social network analysis. We use this to monitor the changes in social organization in open source bug handling communities. We analyze different communities and show how centrality measures capture the distinction in their structure and dynamics. We complement the quantification using a few snapshots of network diagrams that help in the interpretation of our results.

### Chapter 3: A Case Study on Centralization

We extend the methodology introduced in the previous chapter to focus on the centralization event observed in the social organization of the bug handling community of the GENTOO project. Between 2004 and 2008, a contributor named *Alice* was responsible for most of the work performed on bug handling. We present complementary results based on social network analysis and report on the interviews which we performed with three prominent GENTOO contributors, including *Alice* herself. We further show how community performance was affected during the centralization period, and emphasize the negative lastingly effects following *Alice*'s sudden departure. We conclude by discussing the advantages and threats posed by centralization and the relevance of our results in terms of management practices.

### Chapter 4: Emotions and Contributors Activity

Based on the testimony of *Alice*, in which she justifies that her decision to leave GENTOO was influenced by communication problems, we apply sentiment analysis and quantify emotions expressed in messages exchanged via two channels: the bug tracker and the developers mailing list. We find support for *Alice*'s claims of loss of motivation due to a–as she described–"[...]disruptive social environment in the project as a whole". Furthermore, we develop a quantitative method to predict the likelihood of decreasing activity due to the dynamics of emotions expressed via these two communication channels. We discuss the respective implications with respect to the management of community turnover.

## Chapter 5: Triaging Bugs with Social Networks

We combine the methodology presented in chapters 2 and 3 to predict which bug reports are worth the processing effort. Using social network analysis, we learn that the *bug reports*' membership to the network *largest connected component* is a good indicator for the quality of their bug reports. Moreover, we also find that network *centrality* influences the outcome: the more central, the higher the likelihood that the bug report addresses an issue that can be fixed. We use in total nine measures quantifying the network embeddedness of bug reporters to construct a classifier based on support vector machines. We use it to prioritize bug reports that are considered *valid* (e.g. can be solved) or defer *invalid* ones (e.g. need more information). We emphasize that our method–solely based on social network analysis–bears great practical relevance, for it produces remarkably high accuracy results, and only requires information available at reporting time.

# Part II: Software Modularity

Part II covers chapters 6 and 7, and discusses the dynamics of software modularity.

## Chapter 6: Monitoring Software Modularity

We introduce a measure known from the study of modularity in complex networks theory (Newman's $Q$ modularity), to quantify the congruence between the clusters of software dependencies and the decomposition of the source code into modules. Our analysis is based on a dataset composed of JAVA open source software projects. We discuss network visualizations as a complement to quantitative results. We argue that our method is relevant to software projects in general.

## Chapter 7: Improving Software Modularity

In the previous chapter, we observe that software modularity can deteriorate during the evolution of the source code. We argue that this incurs extra management costs and propose a methodology to restore software modularity. Our approach is based on a technique known as *refactoring*. We use a stochastic algorithm, controlled by a temperature parameter, to redistribute JAVA *classes* between *packages* (modules) such that modularity–expressed in terms of Newman's $Q$ modularity–is maximized. We show that the worse the software modularity of a given project, the higher the modularity gain achieved by our algorithm. We discuss our methodology with respect to statistical physics concepts and their implications. Finally, our methodology is implemented as an ECLIPSE plugin which can be freely downloaded from an online software repository.

## Chapter 8: Conclusion and Outlook

We list the contributions of this thesis, framing the respective message according to different areas. We outline future research and present concluding thoughts.

# Chapter 1

# Introduction

"Поехали!" (Let's go!)

YURI GAGARIN

## 1.1 Complex, Not Simply Complicated

Complexity is what prevents us from predicting when the BITCOIN price [32] will crash using the equations that determine the dynamics and initial conditions of all atoms in the market [67, 68]. This example expresses that there are limits to what can be achieved via *reductionist* approaches [187]. As remarked by the physics nobelist *P.W. Anderson*, "The ability to reduce everything to simple fundamental laws does not imply the ability to start from those laws and reconstruct the universe.[...] Instead, at each level of complexity entirely new properties appear[...]" [6]. Within this context, *Aristotle* was right: *the whole is more than the sum of its parts*[1]. This indicates that complexity is strongly related to nonlinearity[2], but it is not quite the same [171]. As nicely stated in [91], "Nature can produce complex structures even in simple situations, and can obey simple laws even in complex situations". Complexity is more related to the former, while the latter is indicative of *deterministic chaos* [201]. What is it that makes a system *complex*, and not *chaotic* or simply *nonlinear*? According to [145], a *complex system* is "a system in which large networks of components with no central control and simple rules of operation give rise to complex collective behavior, sophisticated information processing, and adaptation via

---

[1] *Aristotle*'s *Metaphysics*
[2] linear systems can be solved via *superposition* principle, nonlinear systems can not [40]

learning or evolution". Thus, a complex system displays collective behavior that *emerges* from the interactions between its parts. Moreover, the *emergent behavior* is not found in isolated parts, it is indeed a property of the whole [118]. For example, *consciousness* is considered an emergent property of the human brain and believed to not reside in isolated neurons [212]. Furthermore, as described in [171] "complex systems can survive the removal of parts by adapting to the change[...]", meaning that the *emergent properties* of complex systems are robust with respect to the loss of a fraction of their parts. Last but not least, emergence is the result of the interactions between a very large number of parts. As an example, an *army ant* colony behaves like a "superorganism with collective intelligence" when composed of millions of ants, but if you isolate 100 of these, they circle around until they die from exhaustion [145]. "More is different", concludes *P. W. Anderson* [6].

Complexity is ubiquitous in our life, and plays a fundamental role at different scales in science [117]: from quantum physics [165], chemistry [227], biology [137, 218], up to finance [97] and the economy [11, 185]. Still, the difference between being *complex*[3][4][5] and being *complicated* is often misunderstood. Figure 1.1 illustrate each case, with examples found in the engineering field. Figure 1.1(a) depicts a multi-stage rocket. Although it is clearly made of thousands of smaller parts (even more according to the model), these do not interact beyond specification. They are simply fixed together, and their operation is determined by a central control. This constitutes a top-down approach (e.g. via ground station, rocket crew, etc). Thus, a rocket is simply a complicated machine, difficult to build and operate, but not complex at all. The next example is by far more remarkable. As depicted in Figure 1.1(b), we are referring to a regular bridge, inaugurated in London in the year 2000, the so called *Millenium Bridge*. The interesting fact about this bridge is what happened when it was opened to the public, and what followed as soon as lots of people started crossing it. This bridge was engineered to resist the elements, but not people! We walk step by step. This creates small lateral loads that alternate direction, according to the respective foot balancing our weight on the floor. On a bridge, these small lateral loads can force its structure sideways. With enough people doing the same step, this alternating load can create a perceivable lateral wobbling in the bridge structure. What happened is that people started to adjust their walking gait to the wobbling of the bridge, via a positive-feedback mechanism [54]. At some point, the walking gait of most of the people on the bridge was synchronized, amplifying the wobbling to such a magnitude that the bridge needed to be closed to the public. It was reopened only in 2002, when lateral

---

[3]difference w.r.t. the terminology use and consensus in the literature
[4]in terms of computer science, the definition of complexity used here is loosely related to *computational complexity*, the latter refers to the computational *time* required to execute an algorithm [130]
[5]it is more closely related to *Kolmogorov complexity*, which refers to the length of the algorithm that describes a system (complexity means that describing the system's parts is not enough) [113]

## 1.1. COMPLEX, NOT SIMPLY COMPLICATED

dampers were installed. Here, complexity is the result of people interacting directly with the bridge, and indirectly with each other. The emergent property is the synchronization of the walking gait of everyone over the bridge, which led to a dramatic amplification of the lateral wobbling.

(a) Soyuz rocket assembly (source NASA 2004)

(b) Millenium Bridge (M.S.Z. own work 2006)

**Figure 1.1:** (a) Complicated system. (b) Complex system, when crowded with people.

The inauguration of the Millenium Bridge provides a spectacular example of how complexity can shake the grounds of our understanding. If even a discipline as traditional as *civil engineering* can overlook the role of complexity, what could we expect from knowledge domains which are relatively less mature? This thesis contributes to the effort of answering this question by exploring the complexity of *software engineering* processes. The rest of this chapter is organized as follows: in section 1.2, we provide a brief overview on how software engineering can be influenced by processes of complex nature, while in section 1.3, we focus on the topics that will be discussed in the remaining chapters of this thesis.

## 1.2 Software Engineering and Complexity

Software development is a relatively recent industrial sector which became crucial as hardware gained in power, reliability and affordability, allowing computer based applications to be widely adopted. According to *E. Dijkstra*, expectations were that, as hardware becomes more powerful, programming would become easier [60]. This was based on the fact that code needed to be highly optimized with respect to the targeted hardware (i.e. difficult to write). Early machines would need to make an efficient use of their resources, something that was believed to not be required if hardware was powerful enough. It turned out that, the more powerful the hardware, the more was required from it: source code grew in size and complexity as new software projects were being proposed. By that time, software development methodology was not as mature as the methodologies applied in hardware construction (e.g. electrical engineering). Due to this, the industry faced great difficulties as it tried to manage ever growing projects. The term *software crisis* [39, 156] was coined to characterize this early stage of computer industry, calling for the specification of methodology and best practices for software development and project management, resulting in the birth of *software engineering* as a discipline [195].

Software engineering wisdom acknowledges that project efficiency and software quality rely strongly on human and social aspects related to the development process [181]. For example, due to the intangible nature of software, the respective cognitive challenges imposed upon working teams are relatively high [132, 172]. Team members are required to interact and share their knowledge, coordinate efforts and collaborate on a large variety of tasks, while attaining to the expectations of the respective stakeholders [36]. The following are a few among the many questions–of social and human nature–influencing project performance: How to efficiently promote knowledge sharing between developers? What are the requirements to avoid miscommunication between users and developers? What kind of hierarchical structures should be adopted and how the work load should

## 1.2. SOFTWARE ENGINEERING AND COMPLEXITY

be distributed? Thus, to achieve a deeper understanding of these aspects and their effect on software engineering processes, we are required to take into account the collective dynamics of the social interactions between a potentially large number of diverse individuals (*heterogeneous agents* as it is commonly referred in the literature) [184].

At the core of these social and human issues lies the intrinsic complexity of software engineering processes. Different from other industries, there is no *physical* aspect constraining what can be done with software. The real limitations are in essence of social[6], economic[7] and conceptual[8] nature [139]. Thus, the diversity of feasible software applications is immense. Related to this, the software industry also stands out in terms of the strong coordination requirements dictating the combination of the products of different vendors. For example, *operating systems* need to run in the specified *hardware*, which are *interconnected* via a set of *communication protocols*, allowing then to exchange and interpret *data* generated by different *applications* and so on. Figure 1.2 depicts an insightful example on how different software technologies are combined in practice [143]. Indeed, the need for coordination between vendors is found in other industrial sectors as well. As illustrated in [139], "train locomotives have to fit with the tracks, and lubricants have to match the design of machinery", however, as emphasized in [139], no industrial sector needs to deal with such "as wide-ranging and complex a coordination challenge as the software industry".

Furthermore, the interaction between the processes composing the software life cycle also contribute to the complexity of project management. Traditionally, the life cycle is defined as the specification of *requirements*, solution *design*, respective *implementation*, *testing*, *release* and *maintenance* [90]. In this order, they correspond to the *waterfall* cycle: each step needs to be concluded before moving to the next one. In many cases, this is not a realistic approach. For example, requirements might change at any time, forcing the reboot of the cycle. In fact, due to this and other kinds of unexpected changes during project development, the life cycle can become chaotic: small deviations trigger cascades of changes in many aspects of the project–the so called *chaos cycle*–as described in [169].

Last but not least, the very structure of the *source code* can take the shape of a dense network of dependencies between software constructs[9], thus by definition, source code is also complex [86, 124, 149, 202]. As an example, suppose a modular system composed of $n$ modules, where each one depends on functionalities implemented in each of the other $n-1$ modules. This results in a network in which the number of links increases fast with $n$ ($\propto n^2$). Thus, the denser this network, the more difficult it is for a newcomer

---

[6]e.g. the availability of human resources
[7]e.g. the profitability of the project
[8]e.g. the feasibility of an algorithmic approach solving a given problem
[9]variables, functions, attributes, classes, files, modules, etc

22    CHAPTER 1.  INTRODUCTION

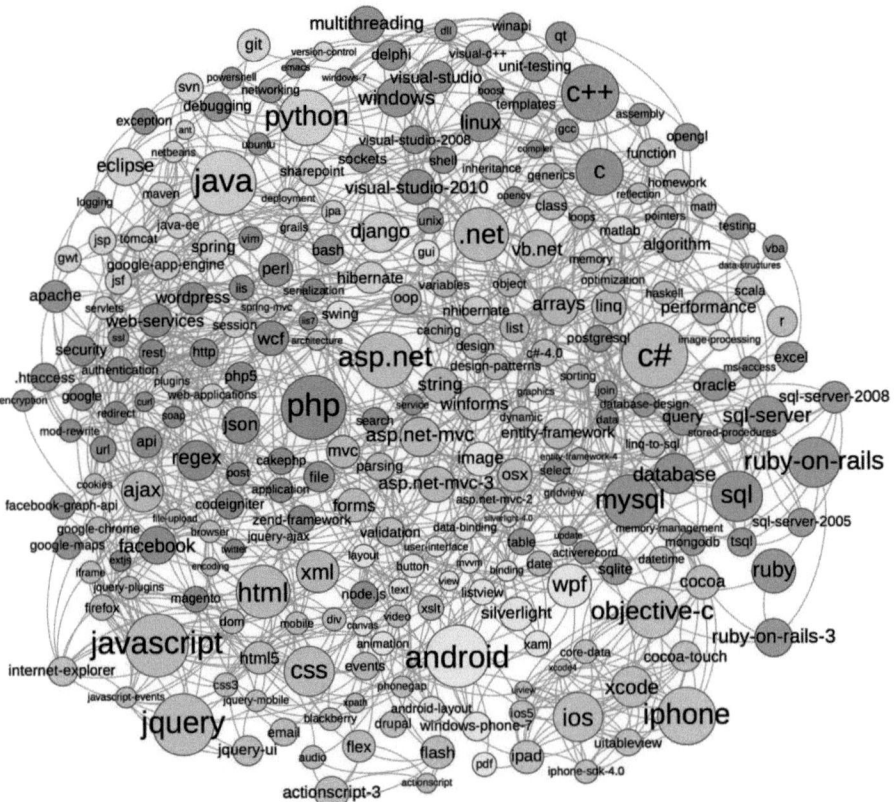

**Figure 1.2:** The most likely combination of software technologies (as of 2012). This is inferred from the simultaneous occurrence of different *tags* extracted from questions posted at STACKOVERFLOW. The latter is a *Questions&Answers* online forum focused on technology (http://stackoverflow.com/). In the diagram, each circle represents one tag. We draw a line connecting a pair of tags if they are found more frequently than what is expected by chance. Furthermore, groups of tags that appear more often together have their respective circles filled with the same color. This is enabled by a *community detection* approach [30]. The resulting network diagram illustrates the potential coordination challenges faced by software vendors (with permission of PIOTR MIDGAŁ [143]).

to understand how the software works, a fact that imposes stringent limitations in terms of maintainability and expandability of its existing functionalities. Finally, the process of writing software is error prone. While syntax errors are easily found by the compiler, a vast range of conceptual errors (the so called *bugs* e.g. caused by poor design, typos, etc) can be overlooked during development/compilation and will only be detected by the end-user at runtime, due to the fact that exhaustive testing is often unattainable [90].

## 1.3 Focus of the Thesis

This thesis has two parts. Part I focuses on the *bug handling communities* of a number of *open source* software projects. These communities are responsible for triaging bug reports. The latter constitute descriptions of malfunctions reported by others and must be processed in order to improve the software. Since resources are often limited, reports must be triaged in order to prioritize more urgent issues, and also to avoid wasting time on descriptions that are incomplete or in general, *faulty*. A great deal of social interactions can take place within the community while a bug report is being processed. We discuss further details in chapters 2–5, while in section 1.3.1 we summarize the respective contributions. Part II presents our work on *software modularity*. We propose to measure the evolution of software modularity using a quantitative approach that expresses the congruence between the clusters of software dependencies[10] and the decomposition of the source code in terms of modules. We employ our method in a study focused on a dataset composed of JAVA open source projects, and show that software modularity can decrease over time. As this can impact management costs, we propose an algorithm to remodularize source code and restore software modularity. We summarize our contribution in section 1.3.2, while further details are discussed in chapters 6 and 7.

As discussed in section 1.2, the contents of these two parts are related to the complexity of software engineering processes. In Part I the focus is on social interactions, while in Part II the focus is on software dependencies. In terms of methodology, these two parts share an remarkable characteristic: *social interactions* and *software dependencies* can be reexpressed as *network* structures. A network[11] represents a set of *nodes* which are connected by a set of *links* [224]. In Figure 1.3(a) we illustrate a social network in which software developers interact by exchanging messages. Figure 1.3(b) depicts a network of software dependencies between files.

[10] use of attributes, methods, functions, inheritance, etc
[11] also known as graph within the computer science domain, such that network nodes represent graph vertices while network links represent graph edges

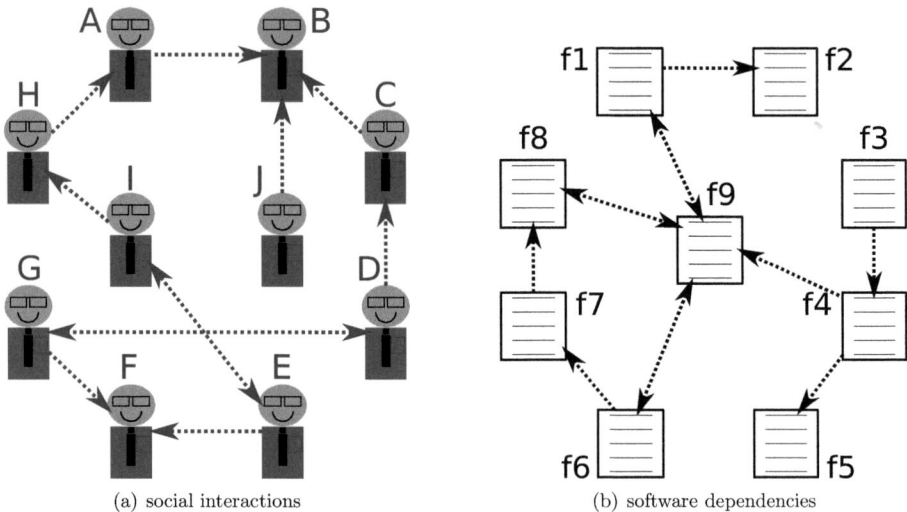

**Figure 1.3:** (a) social network: e.g. developer **A** sends a message to developer **B**. (b) software network: e.g. file **f1** uses a function implemented in file **f2**.

Networks are extremely useful in practice as they enable the use of quantitative methods to study complexity. With networks, a complex system can be analysed as whole, allowing us to minimize the use of complementary reductionist approaches. This methodology was developed within the context of mathematics and computer science, and was recently rediscovered in statistical physics [4, 151]. In current literature, this methodology is known as *complex networks theory*. The field is growing fast, due the availability of computational power and due to its relevance with respect to the wide spread of INTERNET based applications and the underlying infrastructure that keep us connected "24/7".

In this thesis, we focus on *aggregated networks*, i.e. networks that are created by aggregating all interactions (i.e. links) taking place within a given time period. Recent developments in the literature state that aggregated networks can be misleading [164, 183]. They show that paths[12] that are observed in an aggregated network might not be realizable when considering the exact temporal sequence of the respective interactions. We argue that the use of aggregated networks does not jeopardize the results presented in this thesis. The adoption of time-preserving networks or simply *temporal networks* can only improve our results, for the following reasons:

---

[12] a sequence of links connecting two nodes

## 1.3. FOCUS OF THE THESIS

- In Part I: We use a short sliding window of 30 days width and an associated step size of one day to aggregate social interactions over a given timespan. This is an arbitrary choice which was found to be very reasonable, since varying these two parameters did not have significant impact on our results. The referred social interaction are illustrated in Figure 1.4. Moreover, the context of our research is focused on social embeddedness and the frequency of interactions, not their sequence. Finally, the high accuracy performance of our bug report classifier (see Chapter 5) provides strong evidence that our approach is adequate within the given context.

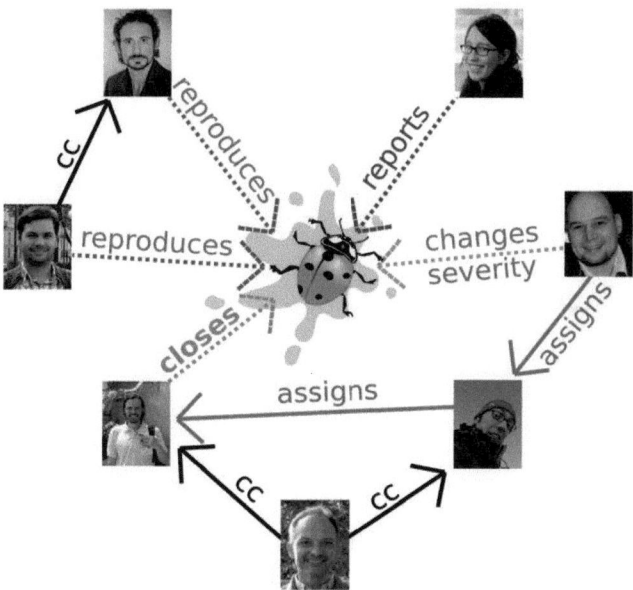

**Figure 1.4:** Bug report updates and life cycle according to BUGZILLA's infrastructure. After being reported, a bug can be forwarded (i.e. *cc*), reproduced, assigned and finally closed. The direct interactions between two individuals (links labeled with *cc* or *assigns*) can be aggregated to form a social network (diagram inspired by INGO SCHOLTES).

- In Part II: For a given release of the software[13], the software dependencies are static. An example is depicted in Figure 1.5. Thus, the notion of temporal sequence does not apply, allowing us to disregard any concerns related to the use of aggregated networks.

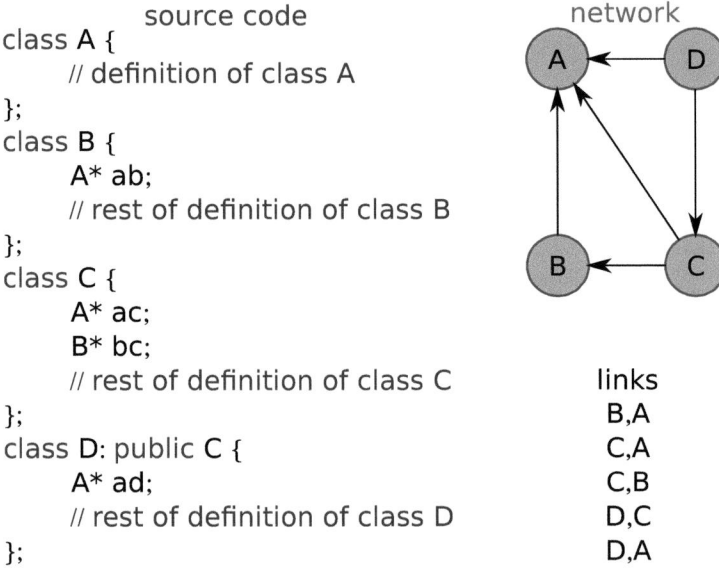

**Figure 1.5:** From source code to a network structure. In this example, C++ classes are taken as network nodes, while dependencies between classes are interpreted as network links (example based on [149]).

For a given aggregated network, we can compute a number of measures that emphasize the different roles of individuals in a social organization, allowing us to rank individuals according to their importance[14] when focusing on a given role. Figure 1.6 depicts how different measures emphasize different roles. For example, *degree centrality* emphasizes the number of adjacent neighbors (i.e. *degree*, see Figure 1.6(a)), while betweenness centrality emphasizes the number of paths that include a given node (intermediators score high on this measure, see Figure 1.6(b)). More interestingly, *eigenvector centrality* emphasizes

---
[13]repository snapshot of the source code, version available for download, etc
[14]in network terminology, we refer to this as *centrality*

## 1.3. FOCUS OF THE THESIS

that the centrality of a node depends on the centrality of its direct neighbors (by means of a feedback process, see Figure 1.6(c)). As a final example, *closeness centrality* emphasizes the inverse of the sum of lengths of the shortest paths from a given node to each other node in the network (the smaller the sum, the higher the centrality, see Figure 1.6(d)). The literature is rich in terms of similar measures [152, 222].

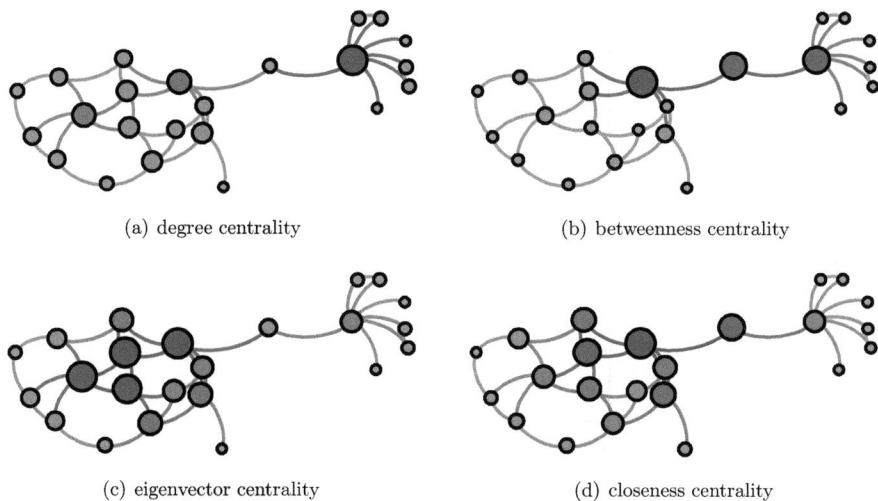

(a) degree centrality  (b) betweenness centrality

(c) eigenvector centrality  (d) closeness centrality

**Figure 1.6:** Examples of node-centric network measures. The node size and redness are proportional to *centrality*: the larger and the more red, the more central a node is in the given context. Thus, different measures emphasize different roles within the network.

In Part I, we apply a number of network measures, and interpret their meaning with respect to social organization. Moreover, by aggregating social interactions according to a sliding time window of fixed width, we can follow the dynamics of these measures. This allows us to observe changes in social organization. This is crucial for the case study presented in Chapter 3, and also enables us to recalibrate the bug report classifier presented in Chapter 5, such that it can adapt to the dynamics of the targeted community. In this thesis, the measures are presented gradually as they become relevant. Similarly, network measures can also be used in the study of source code evolution. In line with this, we present our contribution in Part II. For a broader and more diverse perspective (in terms of quantitative measures), we refer to [25]. They study the dynamics of a number of measures applied to the source code of several open source projects. They construct networks in which nodes represent *software functions*, and links represent *function calls*. Interestingly, they show that the *centrality* of nodes is indicative of the severity of eventual *bugs*. This finding bears great relevance to the problem of *bug prediction*, which seeks for approaches enabling the automated detection of software problems [55]. We argue that the combination of complementary network perspectives has much to offer in software engineering research. We believe that our methodology for automatic bug report classification can be combined with bug prediction approaches improving the *state of the art* in this topic, thus standing as an interesting subject for future research.

The increasingly use of quantitative approaches based on networks stands as a significant complement to the software engineering literature. Specifically in the study of the role of human and social aspects in software engineering, which is traditionally based on a well established qualitative foundation [3, 190]. Current research is now aiming at unifying social and technical aspects of software engineering and we argue that the complex systems approach, with its quantitative methods based on networks, is a promising framework. Evidence for this can be found in the literature covering the topic of socio-technical congruence [27, 28, 29, 36, 37, 43, 128, 194, 216, 217]. We further discuss these issues in Chapter 8, with the concluding thoughts that close this thesis. In a broader sense, this interest on quantification–the main topic of this thesis–is justifiable, as it is essential for an actionable understanding of the phenomena under examination. In other words, it allows us to pinpoint the driving forces and unveil the respective *knobs* that control the dynamics. Therefore, quantification is not only of academic interest as it also bears great relevance to the industry. In the next, we summarize our contributions.

### 1.3.1 Contributions: Part I - Collaborative Bug Handling

In this part we focus on time stamped social interactions taking place within the bug handling communities of open source software projects.

#### Chapter 2 - Quantifying Social Organization

We propose a quantitative methodology based on social network analysis to monitor the dynamics of social organization within bug handling communities. We demonstrate its potential with the longitudinal analysis of 14 large open source software projects covering at least 10 years of activity. We argue about its value as tool for project managers.

## 1.3. FOCUS OF THE THESIS 29

**Chapter 3 - A Case Study on Centralization**

We extend the methodology presented in Chapter 2, and focus on the GENTOO project for we observe dramatic changes in the social organization of its bug handling community. Our methodology shows that most of the work load between 2004–2008 was concentrated on single individual (referred to as *Alice*). We further observe that during this period of centralization, performance–measured as the ratio between reported and resolved bugs, as well the time to first reply and the total time to provide a resolution to a bug report–was minimized. Interestingly, we detect the sudden departure of *Alice*. Community dynamics changed drastically after this event. We interview three prominent GENTOO contributors– including *Alice*–which confirm our quantitative findings. To the best of our knowledge, this is the first report in the literature of collaborative software engineering, presenting a case of centralization with associated account of changes in team performance.

**Chapter 4 - Emotions and Contributors Activity**

In Chapter 3, we report on *Alice*'s justification for her sudden departure from GENTOO. According to her words, she left the project due to a "[...]disruptive social environment in the project as a whole". We investigate her statement with quantitative methods based on *sentiment analysis*. We focus on two disjoint data sets: the developers mailing list and the bug tracker. We find that the threads of messages in which she participated were indeed more negative than the threads in which she did not participate. Inspired by this finding, we develop a methodology that predict community turnover based on emotional expression within textual communication channels.

**Chapter 5 - Triaging Bugs with Social Networks**

We combine the results presented in chapters 2 and 3, to create a bug report classifier that yields remarkable high accuracy results. We use this to prioritize bug reports based on the likelihood that they will lead to a productive resolution, thus allowing the project to allocate resources more efficiently. This only takes into account the social embeddedness of the bug reporter, and only requires information available at reporting time, thus bearing great relevance in practice. We develop the methodology and test its performance using a longitudinal dataset containing the records of 4 large open source projects: ECLIPSE, NETBEANS, FIREFOX and THUNDERBIRD.

## 1.3.2 Contributions: Part II - Software Modularity

In this part we focus on the growth of source code and the dynamics of software modularity.

### Chapter 6 - Monitoring Software Modularity

We express source code in terms of network structures and propose to investigate how software modularity changes over time. We focus on 28 JAVA open source software projects and perform a longitudinal analysis. We apply a quantitative method developed in the context of complex networks to measure the congruence between the clusters of software dependencies and their decomposition in terms of modules. We observe a number of projects in which modularity deteriorates over time. We argue that developers of frameworks should strive for the opposite, maintaining well structured architectures that allow easy adoption.

### Chapter 7 - Improving Software Modularity

We complement the work presented in Chapter 6 by proposing a methodology to restore software modularity. We develop a stochastic algorithm based on a well known technique for source code restructuring known as *refactoring*. This consists of moving software constructs between modules so that modularity–as expressed by Newman's $Q$ measure– is maximized. We analyze its performances using a dataset containing the source code evolution of a number of open source software projects. We draw a number of parallels to the literature of statistical physics, which we believe provide valuable insights with respect to our results. We argue about the many possible uses of our approach and we make it freely available by implementing our method as an ECLIPSE plugin. It can be downloaded from an online software repository.

# Part I

# Collaborative Bug Handling

"The only good bug is a dead bug"

U<small>NKNOWN</small> B<small>UENOS</small> A<small>IRES</small> <small>SURVIVOR</small>
*Starship Troopers* (1997)

# Chapter 2

# Quantifying Social Organization

### Summary

The success of open source projects crucially depends on the voluntary work of a sufficiently large community of contributors. Apart from the mere size of the community, interesting questions arise when looking at the *evolution of structural features* of collaborations between contributors. In this chapter, we discuss several network analytic proxies that can be used to quantify different aspects of the social organization in social collaboration networks. We particularly focus on measures that can be related to the cohesiveness of the communities, the distribution of responsibilities and the resilience against turnover of contributors. We present a comparative analysis on a large-scale dataset. This covers the full history of collaborations between contributors of the bug handling communities of 14 major open source software projects. Our analysis covers both aggregate and time-evolving measures and highlights differences in the social organization across communities.

## 2.1 Introduction

What are the most important social factors that lead to successful and sustainable open source software (OSS) projects? According to *Linus' Law*–which states that "given enough eyeballs, all bugs are shallow" [170]–the quality and success of OSS projects critically depends on the existence of a sufficiently large community of contributors[1] who review, modify and improve the publicly available source code. Apart from development efforts, another important success factor is the existence of a stable community of contributors who report software defects, request and inspire new features, reproduce bugs or comment on issues reported by other contributors. By employing the collective knowledge and diverse experiences of many contributors, most OSS communities manage to provide technical assistance to a less experienced audience, often on a time scale that is competitive to commercial software support.

Depending on the distribution of competencies and responsibilities of contributors, largely different patterns of collaborations may arise. While it is generally difficult to assess these social factors of OSS projects, the availability of large scale data on community dynamics increasingly allows to study the *social dimension of OSS projects* from a quantitative perspective [173, 245]. Previous studies have mainly focused on rather simple proxies of social dynamics like the evolution of the number of contributors and contributions or the time span of contributors' activity and were mostly based on a rather limited set of snapshots of a single project. Using a large scale dataset of time-stamped social interactions that has been collected from the bug-tracker system of 14 major OSS projects, in this chapter we study the *fine-grained evolution of structural features of networks of contributors' collaborations*. We thus take a *network perspective on OSS communities* and highlight differences in the social organization of software projects that can be related to their activity, their cohesion as well as their resilience against fluctuations in the community. By applying standard measures from social network analysis we particularly quantify how tightly contributors collaborate, how uniformly responsibilities are distributed and how resilient collaboration topologies are against the loss of (central) contributors. While similar tools have been applied to OSS projects before [43, 112, 154], to the best of our knowledge, this chapter presents one of the first studies which apply these network analytic measures on a dataset that covers the full, fine-grained bug handling history of 14 well-established and successful OSS projects.

---

[1] any person that helps in improving an OSS project in general terms (not a *free rider*)

## 2.2 Social Organization: A Network Perspective

In order to make substantiated statements about the structure and dynamics of the social organization of OSS bug handling communities, we collected data on the history of contributor collaborations recorded by the BUGZILLA installation of 14 well-established OSS projects. BUGZILLA[191] is an open source bug tracking system which is utilized by contributors alike to report bugs, keep track of open issues and feature requests and comment on issues reported by others. Since the BUGZILLA installations of OSS projects are used to foster collaboration within the community, it constitutes a valuable source of data that allows us to track social interactions between contributors.

### 2.2.1 Building Social Networks from Bug Reports

Data in the BUGZILLA database are arranged around the notion of *bug reports*. Each bug report has a set of fields describing aspects like the contributor who initially filed the bug report, its current status (e.g. *pending, reproduced, solved*, etc), to whom the responsibility to provide a fix has been assigned, attachments which may be used to reproduce or resolve the issue, comments and hints by other contributors, or a list of contributors which shall be informed about future updates. Apart from an initial bug report, BUGZILLA additionally stores the full history of all updates to any of the fields of a bug report. Each of these change records includes a time stamp, the unique *ID* of the contributor performing the change as well as the new values of the modified fields. We focus on two modified fields: the field that indicates which contributor is assigned responsibility to fix an issue (henceforth called the *ASSIGNEE* field) and the field containing the list of contributors to whom future updates of the bug report shall be sent via *E-Mail* (henceforth called the *CC* field). We consider any updates in the *CC* and *ASSIGNEE* field of a bug report as a time-stamped link from the contributor who performed the update to the contributors who were added to the *CC* list or to the contributor indicated in the *ASSIGNEE* field, respectively.

Based on the data extraction procedure described above, we obtain a large set of time-stamped interactions between pairs of contributors. For most of the projects considered, the BUGZILLA history from which we extract the network is longer than ten years. In social networks aggregated over such long periods of time, most of the contributors represented by nodes have never been active within the same time period. This fact limits the expressiveness of the network structure in terms of a project's "social organization". In order to overcome this issue, we perform a *dynamic network analysis* by defining a sequence of *monthly collaboration networks* based on the time stamps of links. In particular, we define a 30 day sliding window and filter out those links whose time stamps are outside the window and those nodes who did not have any interactions within the corresponding time period. By progressively advancing the start date of the 30 days sliding window by one day increments, we obtain a sequence of collaboration networks that allows us to study the structure of the community's social organization as well as its evolution over time. Naturally, most of the monthly networks obtained in the way described above will not be fully connected. Since the network analytic measures we intend to apply assume connected topologies, we perform a component analysis on all snapshots and restrict our quantitative analysis to the largest connected component (LCC). In order to test the significance of our findings we further compute the fraction of those nodes who are part of the largest connected component. Table 2.1 shows the 14 OSS projects that are included in our dataset along with the time period and the total number of bug reports and updates that we consider in our analysis. Furthermore, the column $LCC/TOTAL$ indicates the fraction of contributors in the LCC, averaged over all monthly snapshots of the corresponding project. Here one observes that our data shows a rather large degree of variation with respect to this fraction, which may be seen as an argument that this measure is an interesting indicator for the *cohesiveness* of OSS communities by itself. Nevertheless, we argue that for all projects the fraction of contributors in the LCC is sufficiently large to make substantiated statements about the project's social organization.

**Table 2.1:** Aggregated measures for the studied projects. From column $LCC/Total$ to the last on the right, the numbers indicate the mean value ± standard deviation.

| Project Name | Bugs | Updates | Period | LCC/Total | Nodes in LCC | Links | Mean Degree | Assortativity | Closeness Central. | Clustering Coefficient |
|---|---|---|---|---|---|---|---|---|---|---|
| XAMARIN | 4552 | 20721 | 2011-2012 | 0.93±0.05 | 46.76±8.12 | 98.15±22.70 | 2.07±0.29 | -0.14±0.11 | 0.40±0.07 | 0.22±0.05 |
| THUNDERBIRD | 35388 | 313957 | 2000-2012 | 0.53±0.26 | 64.82±53.49 | 86.44±80.05 | 1.05±0.42 | -0.23±0.17 | 0.40±0.27 | 0.04±0.05 |
| LIBREOFFICE | 8916 | 78341 | 2010-2012 | 0.78±0.11 | 73.83±32.06 | 114.41±49.10 | 1.56±0.26 | -0.20±0.10 | 0.40±0.09 | 0.13±0.06 |
| MAGEIA | 6600 | 46921 | 2006-2012 | 0.93±0.07 | 77.54±21.80 | 156.00±59.24 | 1.95±0.30 | -0.37±0.12 | 0.54±0.09 | 0.14±0.04 |
| MANDRIVA | 60546 | 368463 | 2002-2012 | 0.70±0.18 | 88.15±60.70 | 142.16±118.44 | 1.41±0.38 | -0.29±0.15 | 0.40±0.14 | 0.07±0.05 |
| FIREFOX | 112953 | 1067914 | 1999-2012 | 0.58±0.23 | 171.77±117.79 | 240.79±180.44 | 1.16±0.44 | -0.15±0.11 | 0.32±0.23 | 0.04±0.04 |
| SEAMONKEY | 90040 | 993392 | 1998-2012 | 0.67±0.15 | 210.39±251.43 | 364.42±482.54 | 1.48±0.48 | -0.19±0.13 | 0.34±0.11 | 0.08±0.06 |
| NETBEANS | 210921 | 1875878 | 2000-2012 | 0.96±0.05 | 269.71±292.07 | 1069.72±1509.12 | 3.39±1.13 | -0.12±0.08 | 0.37±0.05 | 0.23±0.08 |
| OPENOFFICE | 118135 | 915749 | 2000-2012 | 0.88±0.19 | 319.01±169.88 | 931.35±591.80 | 2.52±0.84 | -0.12±0.10 | 0.34±0.15 | 0.12±0.06 |
| GENTOO | 140216 | 661783 | 2002-2012 | 0.80±0.07 | 338.97±110.86 | 617.73±211.92 | 1.82±0.27 | -0.29±0.10 | 0.49±0.13 | 0.04±0.03 |
| KDE | 179470 | 648331 | 2002-2012 | 0.75±0.12 | 361.16±246.16 | 424.61±301.20 | 1.15±0.07 | -0.16±0.07 | 0.32±0.07 | 0.01±0.01 |
| ECLIPSE | 356415 | 2594385 | 2001-2012 | 0.78±0.08 | 472.58±180.71 | 964.47±411.94 | 2.06±0.38 | 0.05±0.08 | 0.25±0.05 | 0.13±0.03 |
| GNOME | 550722 | 2751441 | 2000-2012 | 0.67±0.12 | 523.76±585.26 | 610.16±616.81 | 1.25±0.22 | -0.17±0.09 | 0.25±0.08 | 0.03±0.04 |
| REDHAT | 414163 | 3777634 | 2006-2012 | 0.45±0.26 | 658.06±865.97 | 983.58±1297.18 | 1.19±0.35 | -0.12±0.20 | 0.30±0.23 | 0.00±0.01 |

## 2.2.2 Network Measures

While the literature is rich in terms of measures able to quantify structural features of networks [152, 222], here we focus on three measures which are able to capture basic network qualities that relate to the *cohesiveness* of a community, the distribution of responsibilities among its members and its resilience against fluctuations in the community of contributors. Furthermore, without loss of generality, we focus on the *undirected network* version of each of these three measures. The first network measure is based on the *closeness centrality* of a node, which is defined as the inverse of the sum of the shortest path length to all other nodes in the network, or

$$Cc(n_i) = (N-1) \sum_{j=1, j \neq i}^{N} \frac{1}{d(n_i, n_j)} \in [0,1] \quad (2.1)$$

where $Cc(n_i)$ corresponds to the *closeness centrality* score of node $n_i$, $d(n_i, n_j)$ is the length of the shortest path between nodes $n_i$ and $n_j$, while $N$ corresponds to the total number of nodes in a given network. Finally, the factor $N-1$ is a normalization constant [75]. Based on this, the *closeness centralization* of a network ($Cc_{global}$) can be calculated by taking the sum of the differences between the node with the highest value of closeness centrality ($n^*$) and the closeness centrality scores of all other nodes. This quantity is then normalized to the range $[0, 1]$ using the theoretical value that results from a maximally centralized star network. Equation (2.2) presents the formal definition, while more details can be found in [75, 222]. In the context of OSS collaboration networks, closeness centralization captures to what degree responsibilities, collaboration and communication are distributed equally across contributors.

$$Cc_{global} = \frac{2N-3}{(N-2)(N-1)} \sum_{i=1}^{N} (Cc(n^*) - Cc(n_i)) \in [0,1] \quad (2.2)$$

The second measure, the *clustering coefficient* of a network ($C$), measures how closely contributors interact with each other in the sense that an interaction between contributors $X$ and $Y$, as well as an interaction between contributors $X$ and $Z$ will also entail a direct interaction between contributors $Y$ and $Z$. Formally,

$$C(n_i) = \frac{2L_{D_{n_i}}}{D_{n_i}(D_{n_i} - 1)} \in [0,1] \quad (2.3)$$

$$C = \frac{1}{N}\sum_{i=1}^{N} C(n_i) \in [0,1] \qquad (2.4)$$

where $D_{n_i}$ is the number of nodes directly connected to the node $n_i$, while $L_{D_{n_i}}$ is the number of links between them. Therefore, the clustering coefficient $C(n_i)$ of node $n_i$ expresses the fraction of links that were realized from the possible $\frac{D_{n_i}(D_{n_i}-1)}{2}$ links which are expected in a fully connected network with $D_{n_i}$ nodes. We obtain the clustering coefficient of a network by averaging the clustering coefficient scores of all existing nodes, according to equation (2.4). This procedure can be seen as measuring how *cohesive* the community is in terms of nodes being embedded in collaborating clusters [222].

Finally, the *assortativity* ($r$) measures a contributor's preference to connect to other contributors that have a similar degree of connectivity (the degree being a node's number of direct connections to other nodes). Networks in which nodes are preferentially connected to nodes with similar degree are called assortative. In this case a positive degree assortativity ($0 \ll r \leq 1$) indicates a positive correlation between the degrees of neighboring nodes. Networks in which nodes are preferentially connected to nodes with different degree are called disassortative and in this case, degree assortativity is negative ($0 \gg r \geq -1$). In a disassortative network, most of the links are intermediated by a *subset* of the nodes. Therefore, a disassortative network will not be resillient to turnover in the latter. In networks with zero degree assortativity, there is no correlation between the degrees of connected nodes, i.e. nodes do not exhibit a preference for one or the other. This can be expressed as

$$r = \frac{\sum_{ij} ij(e_{i,j} - q_i^2)}{\sigma(q)^2} \in [-1,1] \qquad (2.5)$$

where $e_{ij}$ is the fraction of all links in the network that join together nodes with degrees $i$ and $j$, $q_i = \sum_j e_{i,j}$ and $\sigma(q)$ is the standard deviation of the distribution of $q_i$. The term $q_i^2$ is the equivalent to the expected value of $e_{i,j}$ inferred from a random undirected network. Therefore, if $r = 0$ the pattern of interconnection between nodes is random [150].

## 2.3 Comparative Analysis of OSS Communities

As described above, the results presented here have been obtained for the LCC of the network of monthly collaborations in terms of *CC* and *ASSIGNEE* interactions. While Table 2.1 shows the aggregate measures averaged over all time windows for every project in our database, here we focus on the projects GENTOO and KDE (both GNU/LINUX related projects) as well as ECLIPSE and NETBEANS (both JAVA IDEs). These have been chosen because a) their communities are of comparable size and age, b) the respective pairs of projects address similar problem domains and c) they represent contrasting examples with respect to the measures studied in this chapter.

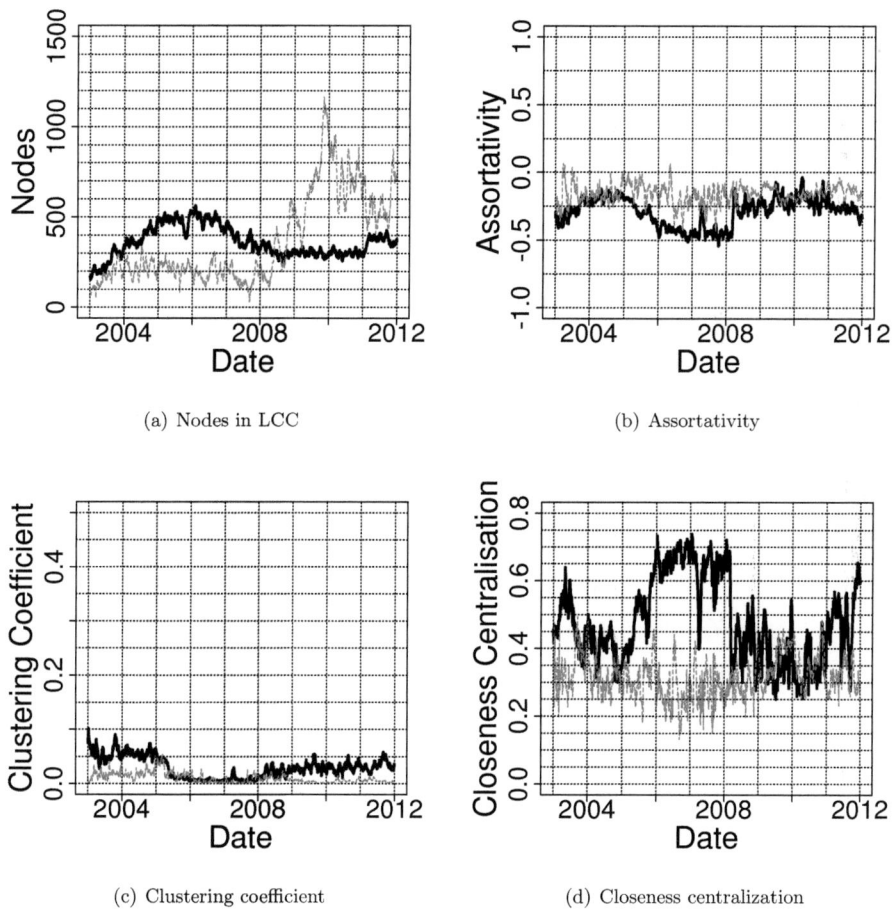

**Figure 2.1:** Evolution of structural measures of the LCC in the monthly collaboration networks: GNU/LINUX related projects GENTOO (black) and KDE (green).

Figure 2.1 and Figure 2.2 show the evolution of the number of nodes in the LCC, its assortativity, clustering coefficient and closeness centralization for these four projects. For all projects, the fraction of nodes in the LCC is rather stable with values between

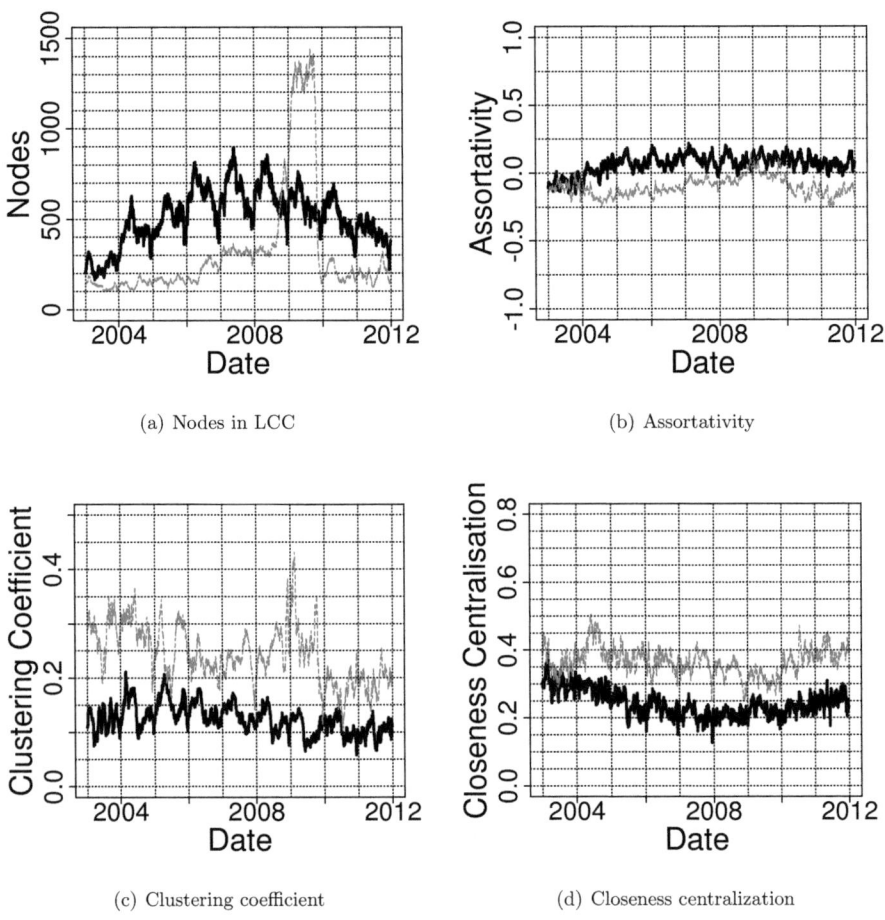

(a) Nodes in LCC  (b) Assortativity

(c) Clustering coefficient  (d) Closeness centralization

**Figure 2.2:** Evolution of structural measures of the LCC in the monthly collaboration networks: IDEs ECLIPSE (black) and NETBEANS (green).

0.7 and 1 consistent with the aggregate values given in Table 2.1. The same is true for the evolution of the mean degree. We thus omit these plots. The four projects show significant differences in the evolution of the clustering coefficient that cannot be explained by mere size effects. In the particular time frame between 2006 and 2008, the clustering coefficient of the ECLIPSE community ($C \approx 0.15$) was roughly ten times higher than that

## 2.3. COMPARATIVE ANALYSIS OF OSS COMMUNITIES 41

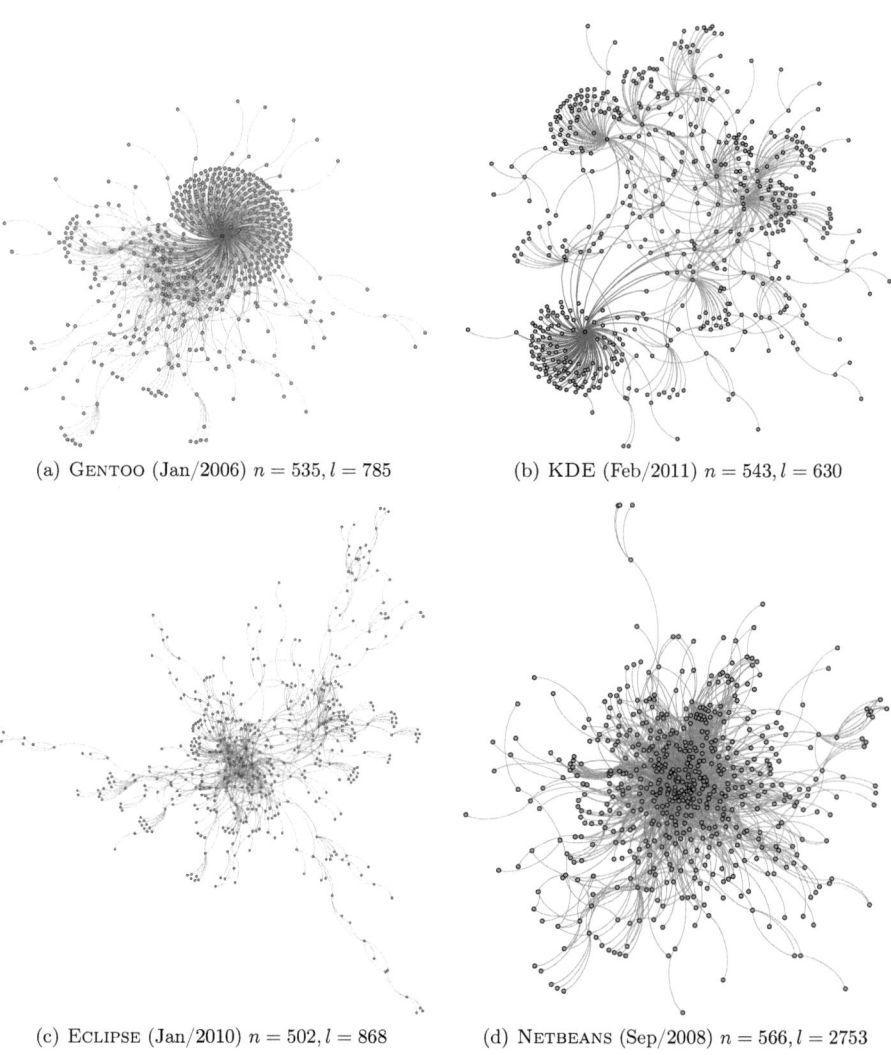

(a) GENTOO (Jan/2006) $n = 535, l = 785$

(b) KDE (Feb/2011) $n = 543, l = 630$

(c) ECLIPSE (Jan/2010) $n = 502, l = 868$

(d) NETBEANS (Sep/2008) $n = 566, l = 2753$

**Figure 2.3:** Four monthly collaboration networks with comparable size showing largely different social organization (the visualization was generated by GEPHI [17]). For each snapshot, we indicated the system size in terms of nodes and links ($n$, $l$ respectively).

of the GENTOO community ($C \approx 0.01$), although the LCCs of both communities were of comparable size (*Nodes in LCC* $\approx 500$ nodes). In addition, the clustering coefficient of the GENTOO community shows an interesting dynamics, dropping to a very small value between 2006 and 2008 and increasing thereafter.

A complementary perspective of the structural changes the GENTOO community was undergoing is given in Figure 2.1(d). We observe a "plateau" in the closeness centralization of the network within the same period. In fact, as can be seen in the network depicted in Figure 2.3(a), within this, most of the collaborations were mediated by a single central contributor. As a counterpoint, the social organization of the ECLIPSE community, depicted in Figure 2.3(c), was structured in a much more uniform way. The evolution of degree assortativity is captured in Figures 2.1(b) and 2.2(b). The level of degree assortativity as well as its dynamics differ across projects. The collaboration network of ECLIPSE exhibits a tendency towards assortative structures (high degree nodes are preferentially connected to high degree nodes, see Table 2.1). The opposite is true for the KDE, GENTOO and NETBEANS communities which show a tendency towards disassortativity (see Table 2.1). We argue that assortativity complements the use of clonesses centralization, as we expect them to be negatively correlated. Furthermore, changes from assortativity towards disassortativity are better emphasized due to the respective change of sign, as defined in Equation 2.5.

## 2.4 Threats to Validity

The aggregation based on 30 days width sliding time window is an arbitrary choice. Although this approach is able to unveil interesting dynamics, especially for the case of GENTOO, we believe that future research should investigate the role of time scale on the dynamics of social ties. Furthermore, instead of using aggregated networks future research should consider the time sequence of these interactions using *temporal networks* [164, 183].

## 2.5 Conclusion

We have presented a quantitative method that capture the evolution of different structural dimensions in the social organization of OSS collaborative bug handling communities. Our analysis is based on a comprehensive dataset collected from the bug handling communities of 14 major OSS projects. We view the social organization from the perspective of time-evolving networks and highlight how projects–although similar in terms of size, problem

## 2.5. CONCLUSION

domain and age–a) differ in terms of clustering coefficient, assortativity and closeness centralization and b) that some projects show interesting dynamics with respect to these measures that cannot be explained by mere size effects: e.g. in Figure 2.1 we observe a centralization event within the GENTOO community (changes in social organization), while in Figure 2.2 we see strong oscillations in the ECLIPSE community matching its release cycle (size effect). We argue that the phase of high closeness centralization, low clustering coefficient and high disassortativity observed in the social organization of the GENTOO community, between 2006 and 2008, may be interpreted as a lack of *social cohesion* which can possibly pose a risk to the project: e.g. with turnover in the group of central contributors, the community could fall apart. Thus, in chapters 3 and 4, we extend the methodology presented above, focusing on the GENTOO community, seeking for clues that can help us in understanding the events that led to these changes and their impact on other dimensions of the project (e.g. performance and community turnover).

# Chapter 3

# A Case Study on Centralization

Summary

In Chapter 2 we present a methodology to quantify the evolution of social organization within OSS bug handling communities. This is used to compare the evolution of social organization across a case study including 14 OSS projects, which include the GENTOO LINUX project. In that analysis, GENTOO stands out with a curious period of increasing centralization after which most interactions in the community were mediated by a single central contributor. In this period of maximum centralization, the central contributor unexpectedly left the project, thus posing a significant challenge for the community. We quantify how the rise, the activity as well as the subsequent sudden dropout of this central contributor affected both the social organization and the bug handling performance of the GENTOO community. We extend the methodology presented in Chapter 2 and augment our quantitative findings by interviews with prominent members of the GENTOO community, which shared their personal insights with us.

## 3.1 Introduction

In this chapter, we extend the quantitative analysis of the structure and dynamics of the social organization of the bug handling community of the GENTOO project (see Chapter 2). Our study is based on a data set covering more than $150,000$ collaboration events recorded by the project's BUGZILLA installation over a period of more than ten years. The contributions of our study are as follows:

- We study collaboration structures of the GENTOO bug handling community by applying quantitative measures that capture cohesion, centralization, clustering and communication efficiency. Our analysis reveals a period of increasing centralization and decreasing cohesion that resulted in a situation where most interactions in the community were mediated by a single *central contributor*.

- In the period of maximum centralization the central contributor unexpectedly left the project. We analyze the implications for the project's social organization, which include a temporary loss of cohesion as well as subsequent efforts to reorganize the community.

- We complement our study by an analysis of the community's performance in terms of bug handling efficiency and response time. Our findings suggest that the performance improved during the active period of the *central contributor*, while her departure had a lasting negative effect on bug handling efficiency and response time.

- We substantiate our quantitative findings by personal insights into the social dynamics of the GENTOO community provided by three long-term contributors. These insights support our findings and highlight potential applications of our quantitative measures in the monitoring of collaboration structures in OSS projects.

The remainder of this chapter is organized as follows. In section 3.2 we summarize relevant related work studying the structure of OSS communities and its impact on performance. In section 3.3 we introduce data collection and network analysis methods that form the basis of our case study. In section 3.4 we present quantitative results on the evolution of the social organization, as well as bug handling performance in the GENTOO community. We further interpret our findings, align them with personal insights shared by prominent contributors and discuss threats to validity. Finally, in section 3.6 we summarize our contributions.

## 3.2 Collaborative Structures in Software Engineering

The question how the structure and dynamics of social organization influences the performance and success of collaborative software development efforts has been studied by researchers from different fields using a variety of methods. Due to the availability of data, many of these studies address OSS communities, which consist of *users*, *developers* and other *contributors*, who contribute to the project in terms of documentation, maintenance of web sites or the submission and handling of bug reports. Members of such communities typically need to self-organize in a way that guarantees information flow as well as a coordinated allocation of tasks and responsibilities. The processes and structures of this self-organization process have been studied in a number of works.

Since it plays a central role in software quality assurance, *bug handling communities* have been the subject of many studies. Compared to the development of source code, in [147] it was found that the bug handling process is based on the contributions of a much wider community. In a recent work presented in [245], this community has further been shown to be an important entry point for long-term contributors and developers. As an important finding, lack of attention paid to bug reporters and fast negative feedback by the community decreases the likelihood for such users to contribute to the project for a long period. This is partly in line with arguments about the negative impact of a too strict duplicate bug policy in bug handling communities put forth in [24].

The collaboration structures emerging in bug handling communities can be extracted by different means. Communication topologies of the bug handling communities of OSS projects hosted on SOURCEFORGE have been analyzed in [44]. Here it was shown that large projects–measured in terms of the number of contributors–tend to have lower degrees of centralization in communication. The authors further call for a detailed longitudinal analysis of changes in the social organization of OSS projects during periods of growth. Our work complements this study in the sense that we a) analyze the dynamics of centralization during a phase of growth in the GENTOO community and b) show the impact of increasing centralization on community performance and cohesion.

In addition to studies at the level of the community, the relationship between the network position of contributors and their individual success (like e.g. the number of bug reports leading to bug fixes) has been studied in [65]. The authors find that both the centrality of contributors, as well as their embedding in cohesive clusters of communication has beneficial effects on the bug fixing performance. A similar finding has been presented in [240], which studies the impact of social aspects on individual performance in bug handling communities. This chapter complements this work in the sense that we study network-wide measures of communication efficiency and centralization, their dynamics during community growth, as well as their relation to the bug handling performance of the community. We further highlight potential risks associated with the presence of central contributors in situations when these contributors leave the community unexpectedly.

The relationship between communication structures and success at the level of teams was studied in [230]. Here it was shown that positive team performance is related to communication structures that facilitate information dissemination. However, no clear relation between differences in the coordination practices and the project success could be identified. In [239], the dynamics of collaboration structures of 14 OSS communities has been studied. Similarly, in [46], co-ordination practices of the bug handling process have been studied for four OSS communities. The authors found that contributions are not distributed equally and that the community is organized in a core-periphery structure. Unequal division of labor and an increasing degree of centralization are compatible with findings about the rise of a leader are presented in [88]. Here, a leader is defined as a contributor who consistently provides high quality contributions, co-ordinates efforts [189] and around whom the community is centered [69]. Usually, leadership in OSS projects is shared between several contributors. The analysis performed in [177] shows that overdependence on a leader results in an unstable situation where the project may accelerate–initially–its development, but which may end up saturating the leader.

The present chapter extends these previous works in the following way. First, we study the dynamics of a more comprehensive set of network measures that can be interpreted in terms of *cohesion, centralization* and *communication efficiency*. We particularly study how the social organization of the GENTOO community evolves during an initial phase of growth and a subsequent phase of increasing centralization that is due to the presence of a central contributor. We then relate our results with proxies for community performance and study how both performance and social organization are impacted by the loss of a central contributor. Finally, we interpret and substantiate our findings by means of insights from actual contributors to the GENTOO community.

## 3.3 Methodology

In our study of the dynamics of social organization in the bug handling community of GENTOO, we use the project's installation of the BUGZILLA bug tracker as data source. We first describe our process of retrieving data and extracting evolving collaboration networks. We then introduce the quantitative measures applied in our analysis of collaboration networks and briefly comment on their interpretation in the context of OSS projects.

Furthermore, we summarize how we selected three community members in order to substantiate our findings by means of personal insights from former and active contributors to the GENTOO project.

### 3.3.1 Data Collection

In January 2002, the GENTOO community started to use the BUGZILLA bug tracking system. The full history of all bug reports submitted since then are recorded in the database of the project's BUGZILLA installation. Data available for each of these bug reports include the history of all updates to any field along with time stamps and the ID of the contributor who applied the update. In the context of our analysis, we particular extract the ID of the contributor who initially submitted a bug report, as well as the time of the submission and the status of a bug report, like e.g. *unconfirmed, pending, reproduced* or *resolved*. For those bugs whose final status was set to *resolved*, we additionally collected the *resolution* field of the report, which can take one of the values *fixed, duplicate, invalid, needinfo* or *wontfix*. An entry *fixed* refers to those bugs for which the community eventually provided a fix. Bug reports whose *resolution* field was set to *duplicate* were identified to be duplicates of an existing bug report that refers to the same issue. Bugs with the final resolution *invalid* are those that do not refer to actual software issues, instead referring for instance to a misunderstanding on the contributor's side. If a bug report is incomplete in the sense that it lacks important information that would not allow to reproduce or fix the underlying issue and if the reporting contributor fails to provide the necessary information within a certain time, the *resolution* field of a bug report is set to *needinfo*. Finally, the resolution of those bug reports that are valid and complete, but that nevertheless cannot be fixed either due to a lack of resources or the fact that the issue is due to an external dependency are marked as *wontfix*. The fact that all changes to the *resolution* field of a bug report as well as the submission of the bug report itself are associated with a precise time stamp, further allows us to compute the number of bugs that were submitted or resolved with a given status within a given period of time. In addition to all updates that relate to the resolution status of a bug, we also extracted the full history of the *assignee* and the *cc* fields of each bug report. The *assignee* field contains the ID of the contributor who was made responsible for providing a solution for a particular bug report, while the *cc* field contains a list of contributor IDs that are being notified about any future updates on a particular bug.

All of the data were collected via the public *API* of the GENTOO project's BUGZILLA installation. In total, we retrieved data on $140,216$ bug reports and $661,783$ change events recorded between January 1st 2002 and April 26th 2012. Some statistics of the data set, including the fraction of resolved bugs falling in each of the aforementioned resolution categories are shown in Table 3.1.

### 3.3.2 Network Construction

A core aspect of our study is the quantitative analysis of the collaboration structure of the GENTOO community during particular periods of time. Even though our data set contains the full record of updates to bug reports, for the construction of collaboration networks, we limit our study to those update events that unambiguously capture dyadic *social* interactions between two contributors. In particular, for each addition of a user ID to the *cc* and *assignee* field of a bug report, we infer a dyadic interaction between the contributor performing the change and the ID of the contributor that was added to the field. We further associate this interaction with the time stamp of the associated update of the bug report. Focusing on updates to the *cc* and *assignee* fields of bug reports necessarily provides a limited perspective on the social organization of a community. Nevertheless we decided to neglect additional data like e.g. the sequence of comments on bugs for which an inference of directed interaction networks is more difficult and error-prone. We rather argue that the collaboration networks resulting from our construction procedure are nevertheless insightful. The fact that a contributor $A$ adds contributor $B$ to the *cc* field of a bug indicates that $A$ is aware of $B$ and that $A$ knows about the interests or competencies of $B$. Furthermore, the fact that contributor $X$ adds $Y$ to the *assignee* field of a bug report highlights that these contributors have different roles in the community, like e.g. $X$ identifying the cause of an issue and assigning it to $Y$.

Excluding those change events where contributors added themselves to the *cc* or *assignee* field, we infer more than $150,000$ directed interactions between contributors of the GENTOO community. The structure and dynamics of these interactions can be studied in terms of a *collaboration network* in which nodes represent contributors and directed links represent interactions between them. A quantitative analysis of such network structures can reveal interesting insights into the community's organization. Rather than aggregating all interactions occurring over a period of ten years, we further utilize the fact that all interactions inferred from our data set are *time-stamped*. In particular, we define a time window of 30 days, filter out all interactions whose time stamps are outside this time window and construct a network from all remaining interactions (see an illustration of this procedure in Figure 3.1). Starting on the first day of the observation period, we then progressively slide the start date of this time window by one day increments. This sliding window approach yields a sequence of $3,765$ networks, each of them representing the collaboration structures of the community within a 30 day period starting at a particular day.

**Table 3.1:** Basic statistics of the BUGZILLA data set used for this study.

| Statistic | GENTOO |
|---|---|
| Observation period | 01/04/2002 to 04/26/2012 |
| Bug reports | 140,216 |
| Change events | 661,783 |
| Users | 36,555 |
| Collaboration events | 153,610 |
| Change events / Bug reports | 4.72 |
| Resolved (Resolved / Bug reports) | 86,352 (0.61) |
| FIXED (FIXED / Resolved) | 39,858 (0.46) |
| DUPLICATE (DUPLICATE / Resolved) | 20,529 (0.24) |
| INVALID (INVALID / Resolved) | 14,923 (0.17) |
| WONTFIX (WONTFIX / Resolved) | 7,959 (0.09) |
| NEEDINFO (NEEDINFO / Resolved) | 3,083 (0.04) |

By analyzing this sequence of networks, we obtain a time series of network measures that capture the dynamics of social organization. It is important to note that the collaboration networks obtained in the way described above are not necessarily connected, i.e. they may consist of different disconnected components. In order to still provide a single measure that can be compared to previous and subsequent snapshots, we limit our analysis to the network's *largest connected component* (LCC). We additionally measure the size of the LCC and indicate its relative size in terms of the fraction of all nodes that are connected to the LCC (also see Table 2.1).

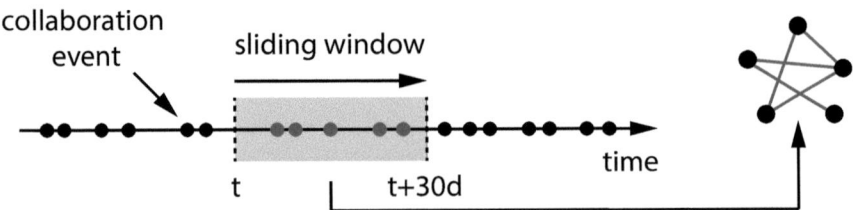

**Figure 3.1:** Sliding window procedure for the construction of evolving networks.

### 3.3.3 Network Measures

In the following, we briefly introduce a number of quantitative, network-theoretic measures that we found to capture interesting aspects of the dynamics of social organization in the GENTOO community. For the sake of brevity, we omit the formal definition of these measures and rather introduce the motivation and interpretation in the context of our study. For the formal definition of the measures mentioned in this section, we refer the interested reader to [152, 222] (some of these are defined in Chapter 2). For our analysis we use their respective implementations in the network analysis package [50].

**Closeness centralization**

The first measure that we applied in our analysis is *closeness centrality*. The normalized closeness centrality of a node can be defined based on the inverse of the sum of the shortest path lengths to all other nodes in the network. As such, it captures the centrality of a node in terms of how close it is to all other nodes in the network. Based on the distribution of *closeness centralities* of all nodes, one can furthermore define the so-called *closeness centralization* of a network. This network-wide measure captures the degree to which the topology is *centralized*. In a (maximally centralized) star network it takes a maximum value of 1 while it is 0 for networks in which all shortest paths between all pairs of nodes have the same length (like e.g. a fully connected topology). In the context of our analysis, the closeness centralization of a collaboration network captures to what degree contributors have the same importance for indirect information exchange. Precisely, in a network with maximum closeness centralization all collaborations are mediated by a single individual, while in networks with minimum closeness centralization community members have more equal roles.

**Clustering coefficient**

The *clustering coefficient* of a network measures how closely community members interact with each other in the sense that interactions between users $A$ and $B$, as well as between $B$ and $C$ will also entail a direct interaction between the users $A$ and $C$. This property of a network can be quantified at the level of nodes by computing the fraction of those pairs of a node's neighbors $u$ and $v$ that are connected by a direct link $(u, v)$. By averaging the clustering coefficient scores of all nodes it is possible to measure the global clustering coefficient of a network. In the context of our analysis, the (mean) clustering coefficient of a monthly collaboration network captures how *cohesive* the community is in terms of contributors being embedded in collaborating clusters. In other words, this measure captures to what extent two collaborators also collaborate with other collaborators of their peers.

**Degree Assortativity**

The *degree assortativity* of a node measures an individual's preference to connect to peers that have a similar or different number of connections (degree). Networks in which nodes are preferentially connected to nodes with similar degree are called assortative. A positive degree assortativity indicates a positive correlation between the degrees of neighboring nodes. Networks in which nodes are preferentially connected to nodes with different (i.e. smaller or higher) degree are called disassortative, in which case degree assortativity is negative. Zero *degree assortativity* means that there is no correlation between the degrees of connected nodes, i.e. nodes do not exhibit a preference for one or the other. In our analysis, we use degree assortativity to capture the contributors' preference to collaborate with other contributors that are–from the perspective of the number of collaborations–of similar or different importance than themselves.

**Algebraic Connectivity**

An interesting aspect of network analysis is that the influence of a network topology on *dynamical processes* like e.g. information flow, cascading failures or synchronization phenomena can be captured by means of so-called *spectral* properties. One important measure in this line is the so-called *algebraic connectivity* of a network. This scalar property particularly captures whether the topology contains *small cuts*, i.e. whether all shortest paths between different parts of the network pass through a small number of links. The existence of such small cuts is known to hinder information spreading and synchronization [225]. At the same time, it can be seen as an indicator for robustness since it captures the effect of a failure of a small number of nodes and associated links. The algebraic connectivity is defined as being the second smallest eigenvalue of the so-called Laplacian matrix, which is defined as the difference $D - A$ between a diagonal matrix $D$ in which the diagonal elements represent the degrees of nodes and the adjacency matrix $A$ of the network topology. The algebraic connectivity of a network is greater than 0 *iff* the network topology is connected, i.e. iff a path exists between all pairs of nodes. This is a corollary to the fact that the number of times 0 appears as an eigenvalue of the Laplacian matrix is equal to the number of the network's connected components. In the context of this chapter we use algebraic connectivity to measure the communication efficiency and robustness of the community's collaboration structure.

### 3.3.4 Interviews with prominent contributors

In order to substantiate our quantitative findings with insights into the community, we contacted a number of long-term contributors to the GENTOO bug handling community. We received three very insightful replies, which contain many details and serve as an external validation for our quantitative findings. We omit the real names of the contributors and refer to them as *Alice*, *Bob* and *Chris* instead. *Alice* was the–by far–most central contributor to the GENTOO bug handling community in the period between October 2004 and March 2008. She was effectively handling most of the bug reports, until she left the project suddenly in March 2008. *Bob* was involved in a community initiative to establish formal procedures regarding the submission and handling of bug reports that were–in part–necessitated by the departure of *Alice*. *Chris* is another long-term contributor to the project, second only to *Alice* in terms of cumulative contributions to the bug handling process. In our questionnaire, we asked for personal insights regarding the following questions:

- What was the impact of the central contributor *Alice* on the involvement of other contributors and project performance?

- What were the reasons for *Alice* leaving the project?

- What was the motivation for the establishment of formal procedures for the bug handling process?

- Was this initiative successful in terms of improving the performance of the community?

- What implications did the establishment of formal procedures have for the social organization of the community?

## 3.4 Dynamics of Social Organization and Performance

In the following, we study the dynamics of GENTOO's bug handling community during the time between 2002 and 2012. Our methodology is based on a network-theoretic analysis of collaboration networks by means of the measures discussed in section 3.3.

Based on the activity of the central contributor *Alice*, we divide the observation period into three periods $P1$, $P2$, $P3$. In period $P1$, between January 2002 and October 27, 2004, *Alice* was not yet active and the community was growing. During the second period $P2$ starting on October 28 2004, *Alice* gradually became the most central contributor. She unexpectedly left the community after her last contribution on March 29 2008, which marks the start of the third period $P3$ in which *Alice* was not active anymore. In the following sections, we show how community cohesion, centralization and performance evolved in these three periods.

### 3.4.1 Community Cohesion

We first focus on the size of the largest connected component (LCC) of the respective monthly collaboration networks. The relative size of the LCC (i.e. the fraction of all nodes belonging to the LCC) is shown in Figure 3.3(a). Since it captures how many of the contributors were disconnected from the rest of the community, this measure can be seen as a proxy for the *cohesion* of the community. In Figure 3.3(a), period $P2$ is highlighted in green. As one can see, there is no significant difference between the periods $P1$ and $P2$ in terms of the relative size of the LCC; it rather remains stable around a value of 75%. However, a remarkable dynamics can be seen in period $P3$ after *Alice* had left the community: After a small drop, one observes a steady increase in the relative size of the LCC starting around the end of 2008. The relative size of the LCC eventually reaches 95% around the end of 2011.

Another *cohesion*-related measure is the average node degree in the monthly collaboration networks, i.e. the average number of contributors, a contributor was collaborating with during one month. In Figure 3.2(c), one observes a fast decrease of this measure during period $P2$, when the central contributor *Alice* was active. Remarkably, it was *increasing* during the periods $P1$ and $P3$, when *Alice* was not active.

Apart from the relative *size* of the LCC, a further interesting question is how efficient and robust the collaboration structures are *within* the largest connected component. For this, we compute the *algebraic connectivity* of the LCC, a measure from spectral graph theory that captures how *well-connected* a topology is. As argued in section 3.3, networks with larger algebraic connectivity a) facilitate information flow and synchronization processes and b) are more robust against the loss of nodes and links. The dynamics of algebraic connectivity is shown in Figure 3.3(b). Comparing period $P2$ against $P1$ and $P3$, one observes that during the presence of *Alice*, both the variance and the mean of the algebraic connectivity were relatively lower. A straight-forward interpretation of this finding is that–

## 3.4. DYNAMICS OF SOCIAL ORGANIZATION AND PERFORMANCE

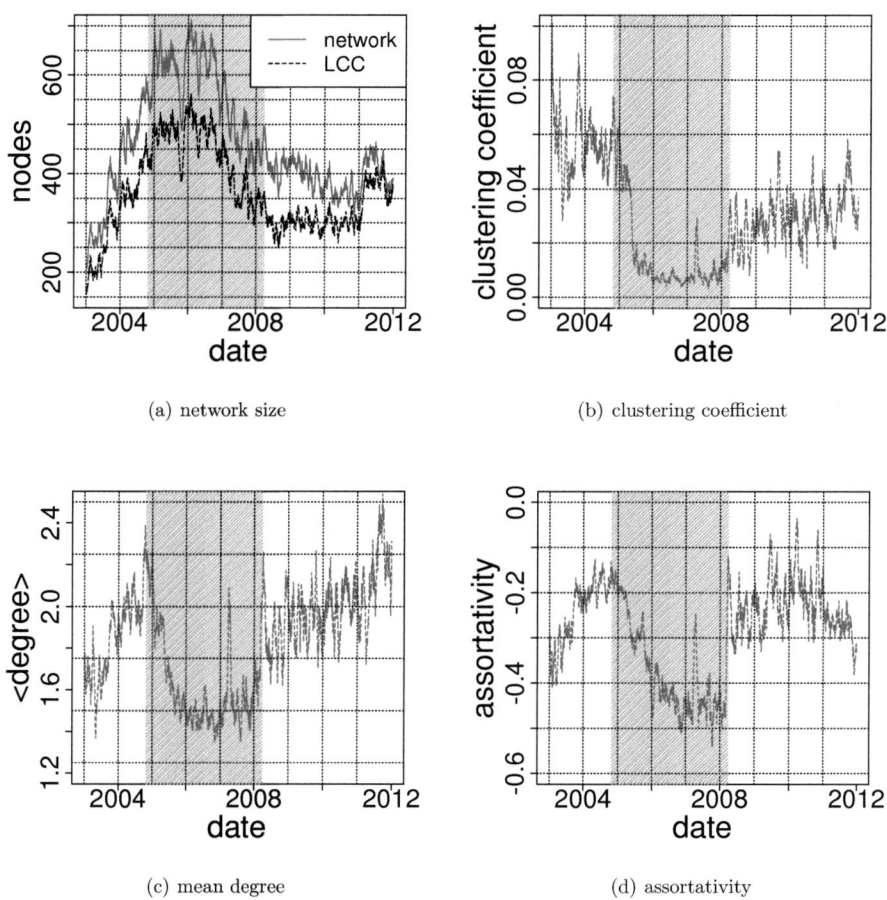

**Figure 3.2:** Dynamics of size and cohesion of the GENTOO bug handling community. Period $P2$ during which the central contributor *Alice* was active is highlighted in green.

as *Alice* was involved in many of the collaborations–the collaboration network's robustness decreased. Furthermore, as most collaborations were mediated through her, the potential of congestion in this particular node increased, thus effectively decreasing communication efficiency of the topology.

Another interesting question from the perspective of social organization is to what de-

56                    CHAPTER 3.  A CASE STUDY ON CENTRALIZATION

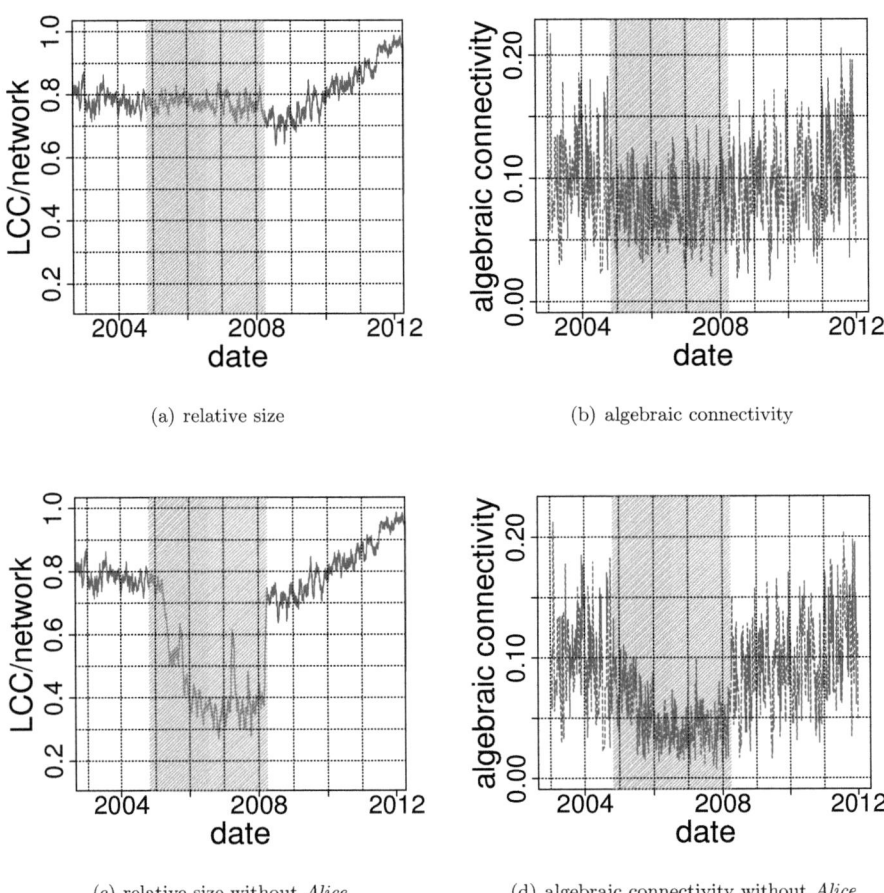

(a) relative size

(b) algebraic connectivity

(c) relative size without *Alice*

(d) algebraic connectivity without *Alice*

**Figure 3.3:** Dynamics of size and cohesion of the GENTOO bug handling community. Period $P2$ during which the central contributor *Alice* was active is highlighted in green.

gree two contributors that collaborated with a third contributor also collaborated with each other. This is captured by the clustering coefficient of a network, whose dynamics is shown in Figure 3.2(b). The dramatic decrease of the clustering coefficient during period $P2$ and the gradual increase in period $P3$ highlights the mediator role played by *Alice*. As *Alice* was involved in most of the collaborations, direct connections between

## 3.4. DYNAMICS OF SOCIAL ORGANIZATION AND PERFORMANCE

contributors collaborating with her seemingly became unnecessary. Another signature of the community's tendency to preferentially collaborate with the most central contributors can be seen in 3.2(d). As described in section 3.3, the assortativity captures the preference of contributors to collaborate with other contributors that are more or less important than themselves. A significant decrease of assortavitity from about $-0.15$ to $-0.45$ can be seen in period $P2$ when *Alice* was active. This substantiates the assumption that most contributors primarily collaborated with the most central contributor while collaborations between contributors with similar importance decreased.

A particular concern one may have in the analysis presented above is that it is unclear to what extent it is the presence of *Alice* that affects the dynamics of network measures. One may suspect that it is the mere number of collaborations involving her that increasingly dominate the community, while the existing collaboration structures are left more or less untouched. In order to avoid this pitfall, we additionally run our analysis on all monthly collaboration networks, however removing *Alice* as well as all interactions in which she was involved. We then compute the relative size of the LCC and algebraic connectivity of the residual networks. Compared to Figures 3.3(a) and 3.3(b), a clear difference can only show up during period $P2$, if *Alice*'s presence indeed impacted the residual collaboration structures. The plots of the relative size of the LCC (Figure 3.3(c)) and algebraic connectivity (Figure 3.3(d)) of the residual collaboration networks highlight that the activity of *Alice* during period $P2$ significantly changed the organization of the community. We particularly observe that–for the residual network–the fraction of users connected to the LCC dropped significantly from about 75% to about 30% over a period of two years. Furthermore, algebraic connectivity of the residual network experienced a significant drop, thus highlighting that during *Alice*'s presence the residual collaboration topology became less connected.

To visually illustrate the quantitative findings about the evolution of collaboration structures provided above, in Figure 3.4 we additionally show four representative examples of the monthly collaboration networks during the periods $P1$ (Figure 3.4(a)), $P2$ (Figure 3.4(b)) and $P3$ (Figure 3.4(c)). In addition, Figure 3.4(d) depicts an example for a residual network constructed by removing all interactions of *Alice* from the network depicted in Figure 3.4(b).

From our quantitative study of the evolution of collaboration structures in the *Gentoo* community, we can draw the following observation:

**Observation:** *During the presence of the central contributor Alice, cohesion in the* GENTOO *bug handling community decreased.*

(a) October 2004   (b) July 2006

(c) May 2008   (d) "b" without *Alice*

**Figure 3.4:** Illustration of representative monthly collaboration networks

## 3.4.2 Centralization

A particularly important mechanism that could explain the loss of cohesion in the community is an increasing centralization of communication. In this section we analyze the

## 3.4. DYNAMICS OF SOCIAL ORGANIZATION AND PERFORMANCE

changes in centralization in the GENTOO community. We not only study centralization from a network perspective, i.e. the increase of the *topological* centrality of *one* particular node. We also consider the effects on the number of contributors that were involved in the bug handling process in terms of assigning bug reports or forwarding information.

We first analyze the degree of centralization in the GENTOO community from the perspective of *closeness centralization*. As argued in section 3.3, this measure captures to what extent the roles of contributors differ in terms of having short paths to all other contributors. The dynamics of closeness centralization shown in Figure 3.5(a) exhibits a decreasing tendency during the period $P1$. A comparison to the dynamics of community size during $P1$ (see Figure 3.2(a)) highlights that the growth of the community coincided with a decrease in centralization, which is in line with the findings of [44]. However, the decrease in closeness centralization in period $P1$ was followed by a significant increase during period $P2$ when *Alice* became active. From the start of period $P2$ in October 2004 until the end in March 2008 closeness centralization increased from about 0.3 to 0.7. When *Alice* left the community, closeness centralization experienced a sudden drop, fluctuating around a value of 0.4 during the period $P3$.

The finding that during period $P2$ the collaboration structures became more centralized is complemented by Figure 3.5(b), which shows the number of different contributors assigning a bug report to another contributor within a given 30 day period. This number is of particular interest, as it captures how many contributors were actually involved in the bug triaging process by *assigning* work to others. Again mirroring the increasing size of the community, in period $P1$ one observes an increase in the number different contributors assigning bug reports. At the end of period $P1$ in October 2004, about 170 different contributors were assigning bug reports. This increase is followed by a *decrease* during period $P2$, again coinciding with the activity of *Alice*. This development was only stopped in March 2008, after *Alice* had left the project. After a sudden increase at the beginning of $P3$, the number of different contributors assigning bug reports remained rather stable until 2011, when it experienced another increase.

From the above analysis, we draw the following observation:

**Observation:** *In the period where Alice was active, centralization in the* GENTOO *community increased steadily.*

### 3.4.3 Bug Handling Performance

Apart from studying the evolution of collaboration structures, our data set further allows to study the *bug handling* performance of the GENTOO community. As the simplest proxy

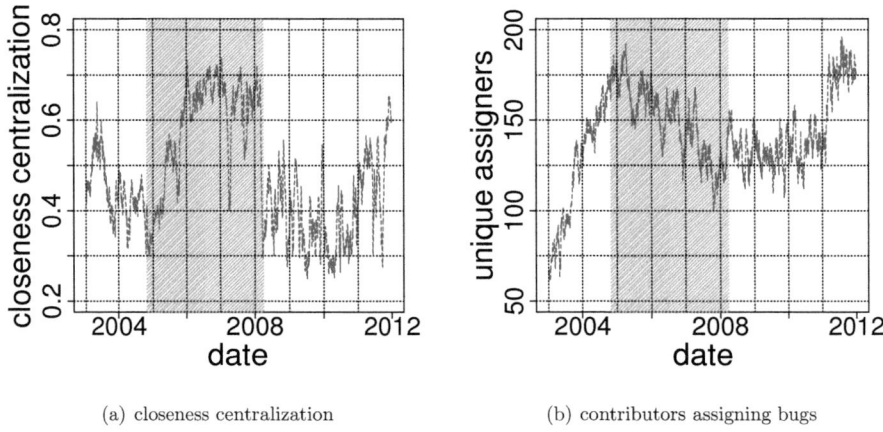

(a) closeness centralization    (b) contributors assigning bugs

**Figure 3.5:** Centralization in the GENTOO community. Period $P2$ during which the central contributor *Alice* was active is highlighted in green.

for performance, we measure the rate at which bugs were reported and resolved. We further study the responsiveness of the community in terms of the *median time to resolve a bug*, i.e. the median time elapsed from the submission of a bug report to the point when it was finally resolved. Similarly, we measure the *median time to the first response* in terms of any update to the submitted bug report, like e.g. the bug being forwarded or assigned, commented on, or its status being changed to reproduced and so on. Figure 3.6(a) shows the dynamics of the median number of bugs that were reported and resolved per day. During period $P1$ one observes a continuous increase both in the number of reported and resolved bugs which coincides with the growth of the GENTOO community shown in 3.2(a). During period $P2$, both the number of reported and resolved bugs decreased, which can again be understood based on the decrease in the number of active contributors shown in Figure 3.2(a). In most of both periods $P1$ and $P2$, the rate of reporting and resolving bugs closely match each other, thus indicating that–on average–the number of bugs resolved per day matched the number of newly reported bugs. The mismatches taking place within $P2$ can be mostly attributed to the peak in contributors numbers, as observed in Figure 3.2(a). These events pushed the work load above *Alice*'s capacity, in terms of how many bug reports she could resolve perday. This mismatch lastingly changed after *Alice* had left the project. In period $P3$ one can observe an increasing discrepancy between the rate at which bugs were reported and resolved, hence indicating a growing number of unresolved, pending bug reports. Furthermore, a remarkable increase in both

## 3.4. DYNAMICS OF SOCIAL ORGANIZATION AND PERFORMANCE

the number of reported and resolved bug reports can be seen around March 2011, although the discrepancy between both remains. This coincides with an increase in the number of active contributors (see Figure 3.2(a)). One possible explanation is that it coincides with the GENTOO community having a regular *LiveDVD* release. As it lowers the threshold of using the *Gentoo Linux* distribution, this can explain an increasing number of contributors submitting bug reports, as well as the increase in the number of different contributors assigning bug reports shown in Figure 3.5(b).

Apart from the mere number of reported and resolved bugs, an important measure of performance of bug handling communities is the time they take to provide a first response as well as a resolution for a reported bug. This *responsiveness* is of particular importance, as potential users frequently use this as an indicator when making an informed decision about which software to adopt ([116, 198] and also related to "Release Early, Release Often" [170]). Figure 3.6(b) shows the median time to resolve and to respond to a newly reported bug in days and hours respectively. Both numbers show a remarkable dynamics which coincides with the activity of the central contributor *Alice*. During period $P2$, the median time to resolve and respond to a newly submitted bug report was more than one order of magnitude smaller than in the periods $P1$ and $P3$.

From our analysis of bug handling performance, we thus draw the following observation:

**Observation:** *During the presence of the central contributor Alice, the bug handling performance of the* GENTOO *community increased significantly, while her departure had a lasting negative impact.*

### 3.4.4 Discussion

We close this section by combining our quantitative results with personal insights shared by three long-term contributors: *Alice, Bob* and *Chris*. By this, we substantiate our interpretation of *Alice*'s role during period $P2$ and the consequences of her presence to the cohesion and performance of the GENTOO community.

In sections 3.4.1, 3.4.2, and 3.4.3, we point out that during period $P2$ the community experienced a significant loss of cohesion, as well as an increase of centralization and performance. We further argued that during period $P2$, most of the collaboration was mediated by a small subset of contributors, *Alice* herself being at the core of this group. Indeed, in response to our questionnaire, *Alice* describes that she "was practically the only person involved in bug wrangling". *Bob* confirms that *Alice* "had been doing our *bug wrangling* more or less alone for a few years". *Alice* complements this picture by saying that the "workload at that time - [if I recall correctly] - was about 4 hours a day,

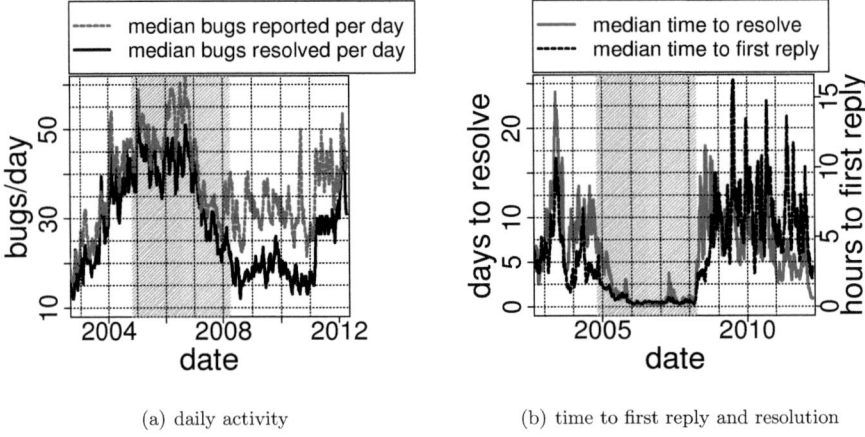

(a) daily activity  (b) time to first reply and resolution

**Figure 3.6:** Bug handling performance in the GENTOO community. Period $P2$ during which the central contributor *Alice* was active is highlighted in green.

probably more in case I did not have time to do the bug wrangling for a day or two". As a consequence of this centralization of bug handling tasks, during period $P2$ our analysis shows a significant increase in performance, measured in terms of response time and bug resolution rate. This finding is confirmed by the community and *Bob* attributes it to the fact that "having a single person on the task greatly helps in finding duplicate bug reports". Furthermore, he argues that having "more [contributors] would water down the quality".

A further observation of our study is that the cohesion of the community (measured e.g. in terms of mean degree, clustering coefficient or algebraic connectivity) decreased significantly during the presence of *Alice*. This is an interesting observation as it highlights secondary effects of the presence of a central contributor on the evolution of collaboration structures within the remaining community. Although it is necessarily difficult to make any substantiated claims about causality, one may conjecture that it is the mere presence and dedication of a central contributor that drives this loss of cohesion. *Bob* indirectly confirms this by arguing that apparently "our bug tracker's users had come to rely on a single person to "assist" them in finding and fixing bugs".

For the community, the loss of *Alice* was perceived as an unexpected event. According to *Bob*, in 2008 *Alice* "suddenly left the project". He further confirms that she "stopped unexpectedly". Clearly, one of the most interesting questions that cannot be answered by a quantitative study alone is why *Alice* decided to leave the community. She answered our question for the underlying reasons as follows: "I would mostly attribute that to a serious loss of motivation caused by disruptive social environment in the project as a whole". Moreover, she highlights her dissatisfaction with "more and more time being spent on bureaucracy, "paperwork", and creating of useless structures within the project". On the contrary, *Chris*–another prominent contributor–remarks that "some people find formalization to be an unnecessary bureaucratic barrier, but when you get to be as big as Gentoo, it's pretty much inevitable".

Independently of the reasons for *Alice*'s departure, the risk of relying too much on a central contributor became obvious in a remarkable event during period $P2$, when *Alice* was still active. In early 2007, according to her own account, *Alice* was "repeatedly subject to [...] disciplinary proceedings and [she] was suspended from the project for a couple of weeks" due to a verbal conflict with another contributor. Around this time, a sudden and short increase in the response time (see Figure 3.6(b)) as well as a decrease in closeness centralization (see Figure 3.5(a)) can be observed, thus serving as an early warning sign of the problems to come when *Alice* would leave.

Despite this early indicator, it was only after *Alice* had left that measures were taken in an effort to reorganize the community. In particular, *Bob* initiated the BUG WRANGLERS project, which a) called for more contributors in bug handling and b) established formal procedures regarding the tasks and goals of bug triaging[1]. In response to our questions, *Bob* describes the project as a success arguing that "the targets that relate to the content of bug reports are now usually met when serious bug wranglers review them". However, despite this initiative, our finding of a lasting negative impact on bug handling performance after the resignation of *Alice* is confirmed by *Bob*, saying that the "goal of responding to bugs within a day is still something to work on".

## 3.5 Threats to Validity

We now discuss limitations of our analysis and highlight possible threats to validity. Since this chapter presents a case study focused on the GENTOO community, we cannot make any claims about the general applicability of our results. Even though our study as well as the feedback by the community provide some interesting hints, we would further like to emphasize that we cannot make conclusive statements regarding the causal relation between increasing centralization, performance and cohesion. In particular, we cannot rule out external reasons driving *both* the increase of centralization and the loss of cohesion in

---

[1]See the website of the BUG WRANGLERS project available online at http://www.gentoo.org/proj/en/qa/bug-wranglers/index.xml

the community. Despite this disadvantage, we argue that our case study is interesting by itself, being a valuable addition to the literature on benefits and risks of centralization in social collaboration topologies. In order to validate our findings, we thus call for similar studies on OSS communities and other collaborative software engineering projects.

Another possible concern is the choice of our network construction procedure as well as the choice of length of the sliding window in our dynamic analysis. In order to only extract *meaningful* collaboration events and facilitated by the size of our data set, we only considered *cc* and *assign* collaborations. Nevertheless, it is clear that taking into account further relations, like e.g. comments, could possibly augment our perspective of collaboration topologies. At the same time, we argue that–even though we have explored different sizes for the sliding window–we did not see any qualitative change of our results. Eventually, we decided to include the results of a 30 day window size, since this period is long enough to include collaborations of more occasional contributors. At the same time, a one month period is short enough to not aggregate collaborations occurring far apart in time. As such, our methodology of performing a *dynamic network analysis* can be seen as a strength compared to the simpler approach of considered a single time-aggregated network.

## 3.6 Conclusion

The main contributions of this chapter are the following:

- We study the dynamics of social organization and performance in the bug handling community of GENTOO.

- We find a period in which the activity of a single contributor resulted in a significant increase of centralization and performance.

- Our analysis further shows that the period when the central contributor was active coincided with a significant decrease of cohesion.

- We further find that the loss of the central contributor had a lasting negative impact on the bug handling performance of the community.

To the best of our knowledge, this study is the first to quantitatively study how the rise and fall of a central contributor impact the social organization and performance of an OSS community. Even though the general statements that can be drawn from a case study are necessarily limited, we argue that our work highlights interesting directions for future research. We would like to emphasize that the quantitative measures used in our study allow to clearly identify shifts in the social organization that are confirmed by insights of actual contributors. As such, we argue that these measures can potentially be used in monitoring tools suitable to augment the social awareness of community managers. Finally, *Alice* testifies that her reasons to leave the community were mainly endogenous with respect to the GENTOO project. Can we measure the factors that influenced her decision? This open question bears great relevance to community managers–concerned with community stability and turnover–and is addressed in Chapter 4.

# Chapter 4

# Emotions and Contributors Activity

### Summary

We extend the analysis presented in Chapter 3 in order to understand how *Alice*'s unexpected sudden departure correlates with emotions expressed in discussions related to bug report triaging and processing. These discussions take place in two online communication channels: the bug tracker and the developers mailing list. Our analysis reveals that discussions involving *Alice* were–less positive within both channels and more negative within the mailing list–than discussions not involving *Alice* during her period of activity. This offers a quantitative evidence to her claims of loss of motivation caused by a "[...]disruptive social environment[...]". We also consider the activity patterns of GENTOO contributors in general. We find that contributors are more likely to become inactive when they express strong positive or negative emotions in the bug tracker, or when they deviate from the expected value of emotions in the mailing list. Our approach opens up new perspectives for quantitative methods based on sentiment analysis and we illustrate how these can be applied in predicting community turnover in OSS projects.

## 4.1 Introduction

Collaboration within an online environment is an everyday challenge for contributors of OSS projects. They need to interact with other contributors to decide about the direction of their project and, equally important, need to interact with users to learn about their demands. Communication within the contributor's community and towards the user's community both impact project reputation and the availability of resources, which are crucial to further develop the project. Thus, understanding how people interact, collaborate and communicate online is an important field of research that has the potential to improve the performance of OSS projects.

The relevance of OSS projects goes beyond research, and reaches wide industrial applications. The current technological landscape is constantly influenced by large OSS projects that generate important software products. For example, the APACHE server is used in more than 60% of the websites[1], and FIREFOX and CHROME have a combined market share of more than 50%[2]. This is possible thanks to the efforts of OSS projects, in which potentially large amounts of contributors can participate by coding, proposing functionalities, or reporting and handling bugs. All contributors benefit equally from the project, receiving the software product and its code as a result. These contributors are free to stop collaborating at any time; a decision that does not prevent them from profiting from the project and using its products. In this sense, an OSS community is an example of a public goods game [7], in which participants have no punishment for free-riding, and they equally benefit from the common good. This poses a paradox, as the game theoretical result of the "tragedy of the commons"[3] [100] implies that, when collaborators are purely rational, the expected outcome of the project is a complete failure.

In proprietary software projects, developers, analysts, and testers are bound by legal contracts that provide a mechanism to cope with conflicts and guarantee a certain level of collaboration. On the other hand, OSS projects are mostly composed of volunteer contributors, whose collaboration scheme can be fragile and suffer in the presence of disagreements or loss of motivation. For example, the PIDGIN project developed a program for instant messaging commonly used in LINUX distributions[4]. After the release of a new version, users, developers and other contributors disagreed on a change related to its user interface, leading to a heated discussion and the expression of negative emotions[5]. As a result, the

---

[1] http://w3techs.com/technologies/details/ws-apache/all/all
[2] http://www.w3counter.com/globalstats.php?year=2013&month=04
[3] another perspective on how/why OSS avoids this: http://www.benkler.org/CoasesPenguin.html
[4] http://www.pidgin.im/
[5] https://developer.pidgin.im/ticket/4986

project was divided (i.e. forked) into two different projects, which is equivalent to a large exodus of contributors. This example illustrates the impact that the emotional climate of an OSS community has on its success. Certain level of positive emotions seems necessary to sustain the intrinsic motivation of the collaborators, and strong instances of negative emotions pose a threat that trigger the turnover of important contributors.

The human factor of OSS projects composes the mechanism that make them possible, but also poses a threat that endangers their success. Often, the social component of the projects is analyzed through social network analysis [47, 66, 104, 240], but the psychological component of OSS interaction has not been explored so far with quantitative approaches. Thanks to the development of tools for sentiment analysis [210], we can quantify the emotions of OSS contributors, looking for relations between their activity and emotional expression. Furthermore, given the availability of large datasets of OSS development forums, this sentiment analysis can be extended to higher levels of aggregation in which collective emotions emerge from the interaction of individual contributors. This poses the opportunity to empirically analyze the conditions that lead to the turnover of OSS contributors, and to apply such findings in the creation of tools to monitor and predict the evolution of OSS projects [48, 217, 237].

In this chapter, we explore the preconditions for contributor turnover. We focus on the large GENTOO project and analyze two disjoint datasets spanning about 10 years of activity involving more than 35,000 contributors. The first dataset contains the records of bug report triaging and processing (bug tracker activity) while the second contains messages exchanged within the developers' mailing list. Both contain textual messages exchanged between contributors. We apply sentiment analysis to these and we study if emotions expressed by contributors in these two communication channels influence turnover in OSS communities. Our quantitative results show that emotions indeed influence the likelihood of a contributor to remain active in the community. We use this to predict community turnover and we argue about its value as a tool enabling timely reaction against undesirable turnover events.

## 4.2 Related Work

### 4.2.1 Social Dynamics of Open Source Software

The social organization in open source communities has been addressed in a number of relevant works. In [147], the focus is on division of labor. By analyzing a dataset composed of the APACHE and MOZILLA projects, the authors show that while coding efforts are concentrated on a few *core-developers*, maintenance activities, such as bug report handling, are performed by a much larger community. In [47], this core periphery structure is studied with a framework based on social network analysis. The social network framework is also the applied in a recent analyzis of the behavior of individuals within communities [104]. Contributor motivation and its relationship to project performance is an important topic, and is considered in a number of works reviewed in [76, 126, 131]. Finally, [36] proposes a framework to analyze the congruence between the technical and the social organization in a software project. In this way, the authors wish to answer the question of which social organization structure is the best performing given a particular technological scenario. Or the analogous, how to structure a technical architecture in order to fit an established social organization.

### 4.2.2 Emotions in Social Media

The most common mechanisms for communication in OSS projects are forums and bug trackers, which are special cases of social media. This allows the application of sentiment analysis tools [210], providing insights to the psychological experience [119] of OSS contributors, rather than just their social interaction. This approach has been proved useful for the analysis of collective emotions in forum discussions [41], emotional interaction in chatting communities [78], and to test previous hypotheses from psychology in online data [80, 84]. The attention to sentiment analysis is increasing due to its multiple applications in finance and marketing. For example, mood measures from social media have been used to predict the stock market [31, 58]. Sentiment analysis has also been applied to customer emotions in Amazon product reviews [83], and to the viral spread of information in TWITTER [162].

Different sentiment analysis tools are available, depending on the type of analysis and data to process. Supervised methods use training data to mine emotions and opinions from text [158], and word category frequencies can be used to measure collective mood [31, 243]. Regarding short and informal text, lexicon-based classification provides unsupervised methods to extract sentiment. The *state of the art* tool in such situation is SENTISTRENGTH [210, 211], which we use in this chapter. The accuracy of its last version has been validated with human annotations of a wide variety of online communities [210]. Among its previous applications, SENTISTRENGTH has been used to analyze emotions about political topics in YOUTUBE and TWITTER [82, 234], product reviews [83], and YAHOO! ANSWERS [127].

### 4.2.3 Social Resilience and Contributor Motivation

The question of how groups are formed and disappear has been addressed for online social networks and scientific communities [13, 244]. This highlights the relevance of trust networks in social recommender systems [219], and how social movements in TWITTER grow and decay through spreading patterns and complex contagion [93]. The departure of individual users, commonly denoted as churn, has also been analyzed for the online communities like YAHOO! ANSWERS [63], and other social networks [233]. Furthermore, previous analysis provide insights on the decision of users to leave P2P networks [107], discussion boards [120], and online videogames [121]. These previous works focused on the relation between social indicators, like amount of contacts, with the likelihood of users to leave an online community. While useful as a first approximation, these analyzes did not take into account emotional expression and interaction, which are related in the psychology literature to motivation and social interaction [98, 126, 131].

The microscopic dynamics that drives the decisions of users to leave a community create the macroscopic effect of social resilience [81], or how strong the community is when facing disrupting periods. Such disrupting events have been characterized by text analysis on FACEBOOK [53], but their influence on the survival of an online community at large cannot be simply mapped to its social network [81]. The intrinsic motivation of the users and their individual decisions are key factors for the collective dynamics of the community. As an example, external incentives do not guarantee more efficient viral marketing campaigns [142]. On the other hand, information spread can be motivated by emotional content [162], leading to higher levels of user activity and interaction when emotions are involved.

## 4.3 GENTOO Datasets

### 4.3.1 Bug reports

The GENTOO project adopts the BUGZILLA as its bug tracking system [191]. It is composed of an online database[6] where each entry is organized around the notion of a *bug report*. A bug report status will change as its processing progresses towards a solution (e.g. *pending, reproduced, closed*, etc). In general, the modification of a bug report field (e.g. status) allows its author to leave simple text comments. Using the BUGZILLA API, we collect the time series of comments, along with the unique *username* of its author and the unique *id* of the respective bug report. In Table 4.1, we summarize the main statistics

[6]https://bugs.gentoo.org/

## 4.3. GENTOO DATASETS

of this dataset. To each of those comments, we apply the SENTISTRENGTH tool in order to quantify its positive and negative valence.

Table 4.1: Basic statistics of the datasets used for this study. We cover activity within GENTOO's bug tracker and within the GENTOO-DEV mailing list.

| Statistics | GENTOO BUGZILLA | GENTOO-DEV |
|---|---|---|
| Observation period | 01/04/2002 to 04/26/2012 | 04/01/2001 to 29/06/2012 |
| Messages | 661,783 | 81,328 |
| Discussions | 140,216 | 14,070 |
| Contributors | 36,555 | 4,664 |

### 4.3.2 Developer mailing list

While handling and processing bug reports, contributors may rely on information exchange through mailing lists. In the case of GENTOO, this is mainly done via the *gentoo-dev* list[7], which is the list subscribed by core-developers and code maintainers. Thus if contributors processing bug reports want to call the attention of a dedicated maintainer, that is the best place to start. Messages sent to this mailing list are stored in a database and can be retrieved at any time from their archive version, which is accessible via a HTML interface. Using this channel, we extract the time series of email messages sent to the *gentoo-dev* list, along with the unique *userid* of its author and message subject, which repeats for all messages sent to the same thread. Again, the textual content of each message is analyzed with SENTISTRENGTH yielding positive and negative valence scores (excluding content commented out with character ">" at the start of each new line).

### 4.3.3 Sentiment analysis

We process all comments and messages in the bug reports and the developer's mailing list using SENTISTRENGTH [210]. SENTISTRENGTH is the *state of the art* tool for lexicon-based analysis of social media messages, in particular for informal communication. It has been validated on test datasets including DIGG and other fora on specialized topics, which are similar communication media as the GENTOO bug tracker and mailing list. When classifying the polarity of forum messages, SENTISTRENGTH has an accuracy above 88% for DIGG, and above 90% in other fora [210]. It has high correlation values with human

---
[7]http://archives.gentoo.org/gentoo-dev/

raters on these communities, providing sentiment scores that would be indistinguishable from a human rater, and providing not only an accurate[8], but also a *valid*[8] estimation of the sentiment. For these reasons, previous works have applied it to YAHOO! ANSWERS [127], TWITTER messages [162], and chatroom communication [78].

SENTISTRENGTH uses a lexicon of emotional-bearing terms combined with the detection of negations, amplifiers and diminishers. Its output is composed of two values, a measure of positive sentiment $p \in [+1, +5]$, and a measure of negative sentiment $n \in [-1, -5]$. Following the rationale of [210], we can aggregate these two values to a measure of polarity. A message $m$ is classified as positive ($s = +1$) if $p + n > 0$, negative ($s = -1$) if $p + n < 0$, or neutral ($s = 0$) if $p = n$ (both having an absolute value lower than 4). Comments with high and equal positive and negative sentiment do not map to this unidimensional simplification. Nevertheless, this approximation is valid in our data analysis, as only 265 messages were found in this category ($p = +4, n = -4$) or ($p = +5, n = -5$). These messages were discarded as they compose an insignificant fraction of our dataset (0.032%).

Table 4.2: Message ratio per polarity within GENTOO's bug tracker and within the GENTOO-DEV mailing list.

| Polarity | GENTOO BUGZILLA | GENTOO-DEV |
|---|---|---|
| positive | 0.28 | 0.28 |
| neutral | 0.56 | 0.49 |
| negative | 0.16 | 0.23 |

## 4.4 The departure of a central contributor

In this section we quantify and discuss the role of emotions in a case study focused on the GENTOO-LINUX project. The GENTOO project is of particular interest due to a well documented centralization event followed by significant changes in community performance [241], which are discussed in Chapter 3. In that work, we focus on the evolution of social organization within GENTOO's bug handling community. Using a quantitative methodology based on social network analysis [239, 240], we show that we can monitor drastic changes in social organization which are usually associated with increased risks. More specifically, the bug handling community of GENTOO came to rely on a single person (*Alice*) to help them in processing bug reports. This is in accordance with previous findings

---

[8]we measure accuracy by comparing SENTISTRENGTH against a constructed ground truth (e.g. average human score), while validity is measured by comparing distributions statistically to check if SENTISTRENGTH produces scores that are indistinguishable from scores generated by humans

## 4.4. THE DEPARTURE OF A CENTRAL CONTRIBUTOR

relating centrality to preference in collaboration [104]. Based on *Alice*'s activity, we divide the timespan of our dataset into three observation periods $P1$, $P2$, $P3$. In period $P1$, between January 2002 and October 27, 2004, *Alice* was not yet active and the community was growing. During the second period $P2$ starting on October 28 2004, *Alice* gradually became the most central contributor. She unexpectedly left the community after her last contribution on March 29 2008, which marks the start of the third period $P3$ in which *Alice* was not active anymore. In the next, we discuss *Alice*'s impact on community performance and the possible effects of emotions on her motivation to leave the project.

### 4.4.1 Effect on performance

During $P2$, *Alice* concentrated most of the work related to bug handling on herself, and as a result, the time to first reply and finally solve open bug reports were minimized (see Figure 3.6). These are important metrics that correlate to the likelihood of a bug reporter in becoming a *long time contributor* to the project [245]. The main issue about *Alice*'s impact was that–due to personal conflicts, and dissatisfaction with the social environment of the project as a whole–she left the community suddenly. As we show in Chapter 3, after *Alice*'s departure (period $P3$) the community never managed to achieve the same levels of performance. Thus, besides monitoring changes in community social organization and implied risks, we wish for quantitative measures that could give an early indication to individual loss of motivation or activity.

### 4.4.2 Changes in collective emotions

To measure the collective emotions in the *discussions* associated with comments to a bug report or e-mails sent to a thread in the mailing list, we aggregate the emotional values of the messages exchanged within each such discussion (a bug report or an e-mail thread). In this way, for the set of messages in a discussion $M_d$, we calculate the ratios of positive $P_d = \frac{\sum_{m \in M_d} s_m = 1}{|M_d|}$, negative $N_d = \frac{\sum_{m \in M_d} s_m = -1}{|M_d|}$, and neutral $U_d = \frac{\sum_{m \in M_d} s_m = 0}{|M_d|}$ messages. These measurements map the discussions to a simplex on the plane [82], where each discussion has a distance to the vertices of a triangle proportional to $P_d$, $N_d$, and $U_d$. Figure 4.1 shows this representation separately for bug tracker and the mailing list, where each discussion $d$ is a point of size proportional to $|M_d|$. The ratio of the overall emotional expression in each medium (bug tracker or mailing list), $\bar{P}, \bar{N}, \bar{U}$, allow us to compare the emotions of a discussion with this ground state of the GENTOO community. We perform a set of nonparametric statistical tests to classify each discussion, consisting on three $\chi^2$ tests at the 95% confidence interval:

1. Test of $U_d \simeq \bar{U}$: if this hypothesis cannot be rejected, the discussion is not considered to include collective emotions, and it is classified as *neutral*. If the $U_d > \bar{U}$ hypothesis is supported, we classify the discussion as *underemotional*. Examples of this kind of discussions are exchanges of computer code or error logs, which serve a technical purpose but do not compose emotional interaction. If the hypothesis $U_d < \bar{U}$, is supported, the discussion contained collective emotions, and the next two tests are evaluated to classify the emotions in this discussion.

2. Test of $P_d \simeq \bar{P}$: if the null hypothesis can be rejected and the data supports $P_d > \bar{P}$, we classify the discussion as *positive*.

3. Test of $N_d \simeq \bar{N}$: in the same way as the previous point, if the data supports $N_d > \bar{N}$, we classify the discussion as *negative*.

The above set of tests allows us to detect discussions that simultaneously contain positive and negative emotions, which will pass the second and third test. We classify these discussions as *bipolar*, representing collective emotions in which the authors of messages are polarized in different emotional states [186]. Additionally, a discussion might pass the first test, but not the second nor the third. These discussions contain more emotional content than the average of the community, but there is not enough data to classify the polarity of the emotions expressed in it. We classify these as *undetermined*.

Our statistical analysis highlights the presence of strong positive discussions in the bug reports, represented by points close to the lower left corner of the triangle. In these discussions, positive collective emotions are usually created as the result of fixing a software issue. The bug report system also shows some instances of underemotional discussions, represented by gray points close to the upper corner of the triangle. These threads are large exchanges of error logs and program outputs, and do not constitute a significant source of emotional interaction.

The lower row of Figure 4.1 shows the collective emotions in the discussions of the developer's mailing list (GENTOO-DEV). The structure of the emotions in these discussions is significantly different when compared against their bug reports counterpart: there are very few instances of positive discussions, and there are large discussions that elicited negative collective emotions.

These differences are possible due to the fact that these two communication channels (bug tracker and mailing list) shows very different styles of emotional interaction. In the bug tracker, positive emotions prevail. Users, developers and other contributors need to interact focusing on solving existing software issues. Thus, bug reports must be written as clear as possible. Moreover, contributors might need to write back to bug reporters in

## 4.4. THE DEPARTURE OF A CENTRAL CONTRIBUTOR

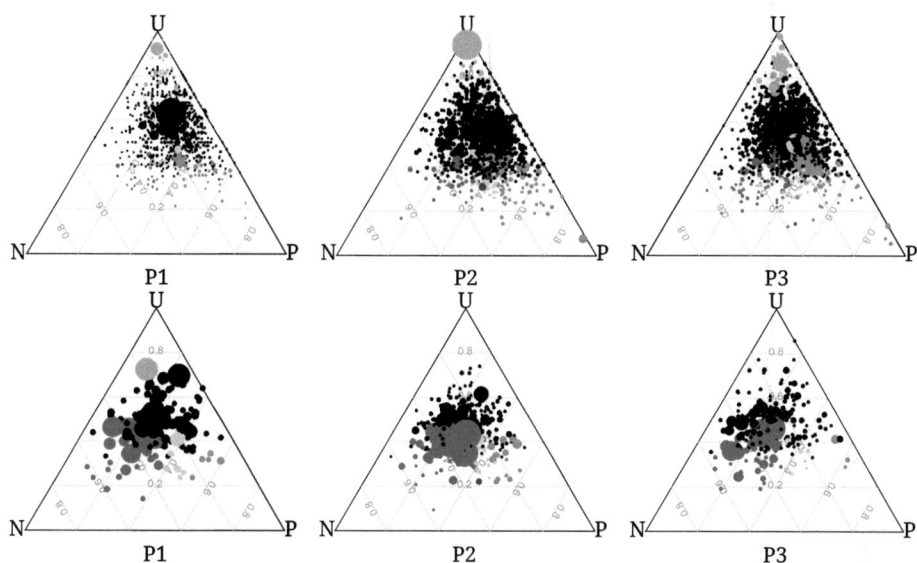

**Figure 4.1:** Triangular representation of the emotions in GENTOO discussions in bug tracker (top) and the developer mailing list (bottom). Points represent discussions with at least 20 messages, with a size proportional to the amount of messages in the discussion, at a distance to the triangle vertices proportional to the ratios of positive, negative and neutral messages. Points are colored according to the classification of the discussion (i.e. black for *neutral*, green for *positive*, red for *negative*, gray for *underemotional*, blue for *bipolar* and yellow for *undetermined*).

order to gather further information. This needs to be done in a smooth way, such that it will lead to the identification of the locus of software issues as fast as possible. On the mailing list the situation can be quite different. Specially in the case of the developers' private list, large instances of negative emotions can be observed. Likely, this is due to disagreements in collaboration processes and on competing agendas specifying how work and software should be organized.

The representation of collective emotions in Figure 4.1 is useful to detect discussions that could trigger the decision of contributors to stop contributing to the OSS community. When comparing the three intervals depending on *Alice*'s presence, it is difficult to find differences in this representation. Periods $P2$ and $P3$ seem slightly more emotional, with some instances of bipolar discussions. For the case of the mailing list, negative emotions appear to be more salient in $P2$ and $P3$, but these observations require a quantitative validation. For that reason, we compute the time series of emotions in messages, using a moving average with $T = 30$ days range. Thus, $M_T$ represents all messages found within such a time window. This allows us to calculate the respective mean positivity $p(t) = \sum_{m \in M_T} p_m/|M_T|$, mean negativity $n(t) = -\sum_{m \in M_T} n_m/|M_T|$, and mean polarity $s(t) = \sum_{m \in |M_T|} s_m/|M_T|$ of messages.

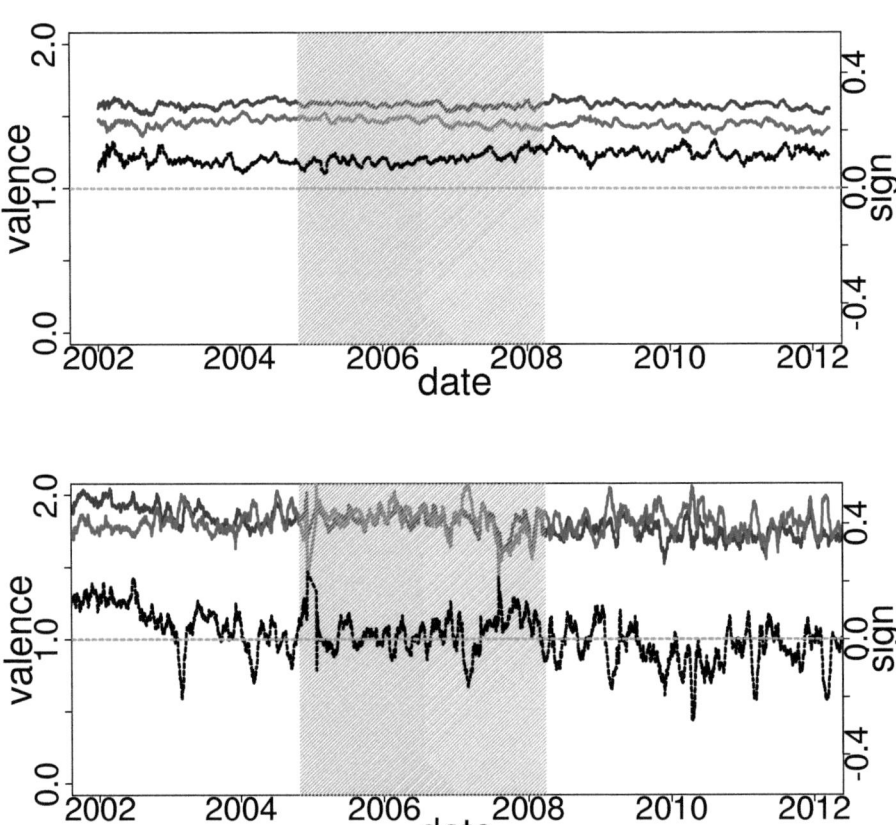

**Figure 4.2:** Moving average applied to the time series of emotional expression within GENTOO BUGZILLA (top) and GENTOO-DEV (bottom). The red curve shows the daily mean negativity in the messages, the blue curve shows the mean positivity, and the black curve represents the mean polarity of all the messages. The green interval highlights $P2$, the period when *Alice* was active.

Figure 4.2 shows these time series for the bug reports and for the developer's mailing list, divided into the three periods mentioned above. It can be noticed that there is no clear effect of the presence or absence of *Alice* in the bug tracker, but the developer's mailing list seems to be affected by her. Before *Alice*'s presence, the mean polarity used to have positive values, and during her activity this was close to 0. After her departure, there seems to be a period of stronger negativity. We statistically tested this observations, performing $\chi^2$ test on the values of $s(t)$ across periods.

The results of these tests are reported in Table 4.3. They support our observation that–in the mailing list–$P3$ had more negative emotions than the periods $P1$ and $P2$ together. During that period, the community went through a complete reorganization, catalyzed by the creation of the *bug wranglers* project[9]. This was an initiative specially meant to cope with *Alice*'s sudden departure. Thus, the negativity observed during $P3$ is likely to be due to the community struggle in restructuring its procedures. What about *Alice*'s presence during $P2$? Did *Alice* experience different sentiment expression within the bug tracker and mailing list? We separate the discussions in which *Alice* took part, from the remaining taking place within that period, and again calculated the different proportions of polarities. We show in Table 4.3 that the discussions in the mailing list that contained *Alice*'s messages were indeed more negative and less positive than the discussions not containing her messages, while the proportions of neutral polarity were roughly the same. Now focusing on the bug tracker, we observed that the proportion of negative polarity were roughly the same in *Alice*'s discussions when compared to the remaining discussions. Moreover, *Alice*'s discussions were more neutral and less positive.

## 4.5 Emotions and inactivity

The above analysis of the departure of *Alice* serves as an example of the interplay between emotions and activity in the GENTOO community. In this section, we extend that analysis to contributors in general, exploring the role of emotions in their activity patterns. We continue by developing a method to predict long periods where an individual contributor is inactive.

---

[9]http://www.gentoo.org/proj/en/qa/bug-wranglers/

**Table 4.3:** Test for statistical significance of differences in proportion of polarities. $N$ represents the proportion of negative messages, $P$ for positive ones and $U$ for neutral ones. The *null hypothesis* is always $Prop_1 = Prop_2$. The subscripts *P1-P2* and *P3* corresponds to the analysis per period, while *without Alice* and *with Alice* to the analysis per thread.

| | GENTOO BUGZILLA | |
|---|---|---|
| p-value of null hypothesis | alternative hypothesis | estimate |
| $1.04e - 033$ | $N_{\text{P1-P2}} > N_{\text{P3}}$ | 0.011 |
| $2.12e - 003$ | $U_{\text{P1-P2}} > U_{\text{P3}}$ | 0.003 |
| $1.29e - 040$ | $P_{\text{P1-P2}} < P_{\text{P3}}$ | 0.014 |
| $2.00e - 002$ | $N_{\text{without Alice}} <> N_{\text{with Alice}}$ | 0.003 |
| $2.06e - 130$ | $U_{\text{without Alice}} < U_{\text{with Alice}}$ | 0.045 |
| $6.62e - 188$ | $P_{\text{without Alice}} > P_{\text{with Alice}}$ | 0.049 |

| | GENTOO-DEV | |
|---|---|---|
| p-value of null hypothesis | alternative hypothesis | estimate |
| $1.49e - 021$ | $N_{\text{P1-P2}} < N_{\text{P3}}$ | 0.033 |
| $5.08e - 006$ | $U_{\text{P1-P2}} < U_{\text{P3}}$ | 0.017 |
| $7.61e - 046$ | $P_{\text{P1-P2}} > P_{\text{P3}}$ | 0.050 |
| $1.61e - 026$ | $N_{\text{without Alice}} < N_{\text{with Alice}}$ | 0.066 |
| $5.50e - 001$ | $U_{\text{without Alice}} <> U_{\text{with Alice}}$ | 0.004 |
| $8.56e - 023$ | $P_{\text{without Alice}} > P_{\text{with Alice}}$ | 0.001 |

### 4.5.1 Activity modes

For the case of *Alice*, determining when she became inactive is a trivial task, as she had no activity after a certain date. This is not necessarily the case for contributors in general, who might be inactive for a long period and then become active again. In general, contributors do not have a standard mechanism to inform the rest of the community if they are active or not, and the only way to detect their inactivity is when they do not produce messages for a period of time. To detect if a contributor became inactive, we use the theory of interevent time distributions [16, 235], which divides human communication in two modes: A bursty, *correlated* mode in which the time between the actions of a human is very short; and an *uncorrelated* mode that corresponds to the long times between bursts of activity. The *correlated* mode can be detected when the interevent times of a human follow a power-law distribution [16, 78], which emerges when humans reply to each other. The *uncorrelated* mode can be detected as an exponentially decaying regime, which can be explained as the result of a Poisson process of decoupled actions that start activity bursts [235].

For both datasets, we measure the interevent times $\tau$ between the messages of each contrib-

## 4.5. EMOTIONS AND INACTIVITY

utor, and characterize the maximum inactivity period of each one through the maximum interevent time $\tau_{max}$. Figure 4.3 shows the distribution of $\tau_{max}$ for the mailing list and the bug tracker, with power-law fits to the head of the distributions. It can be noticed that these power-law regimes are not valid after a certain value, where both distributions show a tail that decreases much faster than a power-law. This shows the division between the two modes of activity mentioned above: the head of the distributions correspond to the *correlated* mode of active contributors, while their tails represent the *uncorrelated* time intervals when contributors are inactive. We found that the point between both modes is approximately $\tau = 30$ days. This indicates that when a contributor does not create any new message for a month, its behavior is uncoupled from the rest and it can be considered as inactive.

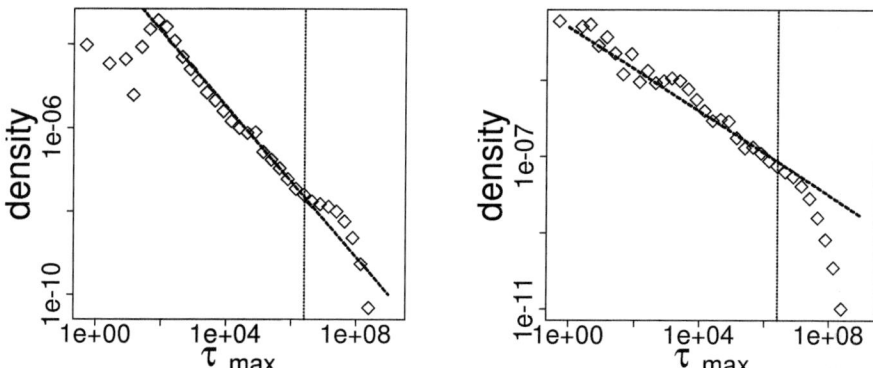

**Figure 4.3:** Distributions of the maximum interevent times per contributor in the bug tracker (left) and the mailing list (right). The distributions are plotted in a log-log scale with exponentially increasing bins, and power-law fits to the head of the distributions. Dashed vertical lines show the mark at $\tau_{max} = 30$ days, where there is a regime change.

### 4.5.2 Contributor emotions

To produce the dataset that classifies contributor activity, we do the following: We collect all messages written by each contributor $u$, sorting messages by date. Then we iterate over the messages, starting from the earliest. If the contributor only posted a single message, we discard this *one time contributor* from our analysis. If the contributor posted more than one message, for each message $m_t^u$ posted at time $t$, we measure the time interval $\tau$

between it and his next message $m^u_{t+\tau}$. If this time interval is shorter than 30 days, we label the interval $I^u_t$ as *ACT*, meaning the contributor is active. Otherwise, we label the interval as *INA*, meaning that the contributor started a period of inactivity according to the theory explained above.

For each interval of contributor $u$, we compute the mean positivity score $P_u$ and mean negativity score $N_u$ of the messages of the contributor in the 5 days preceding the interval. This way, each data point is an interval between messages of the same contributor, with real-time measurements of the emotions expressed by that contributor in the days before the interval takes place. Our aim is to provide a predictor that identifies when a contributor is going to become inactive, as a tool that can warn community managers about the risk of losing contributors. This is not a simple task, as the ratios of each type of interval are very unevenly distributed. The prior probability of an interval being labeled as *INA* is 0.088 in the bug tracker, and 0.075 in the mailing list.

We calculate the conditional distributions of emotions given the label of an interval, $P(N_u|I)$ and $P(P_u|I)$, which we show in Figure 4.4 for both datasets. An initial inspection shows the differences between the expression of emotions when a contributor is going to become inactive and when not. For both datasets, the distribution of emotional expression followed by an interval labeled as *INA* has larger variance than when followed by intervals labeled as *ACT*, showing signs of bimodality. Wilcoxon tests reveal that the conditional distributions of both emotions in the bug tracker are significantly different ($p < 1e-15$). In the mailing list, this is the case only for $N_u$ ($p < 1e-15$), while the null hypothesis could not be rejected ($p = 0.21$) for $P_u$. This highlights the role of negative expression among developers, which differs more when one is going to become inactive, in comparison with active periods. Nevertheless, for the case of the mailing list, the failure to reject the null hypothesis for $P_u$ does not imply that it is not informative, as we show below.

### 4.5.3 Activity tendencies

A notable difference in the distributions of Figure 4.4 is the range where $P(N_u|I = \text{INA}) > P(N_u|I = \text{ACT})$ and $P(P_u|I = \text{INA}) > P(P_u|I = \text{ACT})$. For the case of the bug tracker, this condition is present only when $N_u$ and $P_u$ are above a certain value (in terms of absolute valence), while for the case of the mailing list, this is also true when $N_u$ and $P_u$ have a sufficiently low absolute value. This indicates that strong emotions in the bug tracker, and deviations from the mean emotions in the mailing list inform about the likelihood of a contributor becoming inactive. To measure these effects, we compute the

## 4.5. EMOTIONS AND INACTIVITY

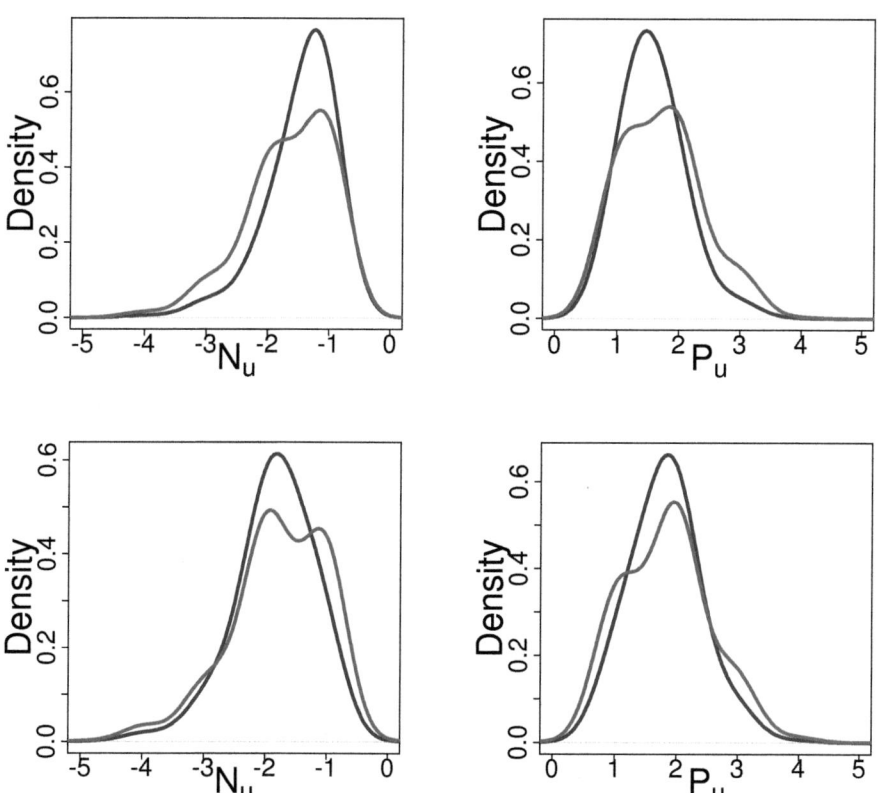

**Figure 4.4:** Conditional distributions of contributor emotions $P(N_u|I)$ and $P(P_u|I)$ in the bug tracker (top) and the mailing list (bottom) for $I = $ ACT (blue) and $I = $ INA (red). Distributions were smoothed through a Gaussian kernel of width 0.35.

posterior distribution of a contributor becoming inactive at given time, considering his emotional expression in the last five days as

$$P(I = \text{INA}|N_u) = \frac{P(N_u|I = \text{INA}) \times P(I = \text{INA})}{P(N_u)} \quad (4.1)$$

and its equivalent for $P_u$. We bin $P_u$ and $N_u$ in five bins, using the ranges $[1, 5]$ and $[-1, -5]$ respectively, computing confidence intervals for the posterior distribution. Figure

4.5 shows the posterior likelihood of becoming inactive for the first four bins, as the fifth one was not giving significant values due to the low probability of having $|P_u| > 4$ and $|N_u| > 4$. Our observation of the difference of the influence of emotions in both communication channels becomes clear: the likelihood of becoming inactive increases with $P_u$ and $N_u$ in the case of the bug tracker, while it grows with the distance to the mean for the case of the mailing list.

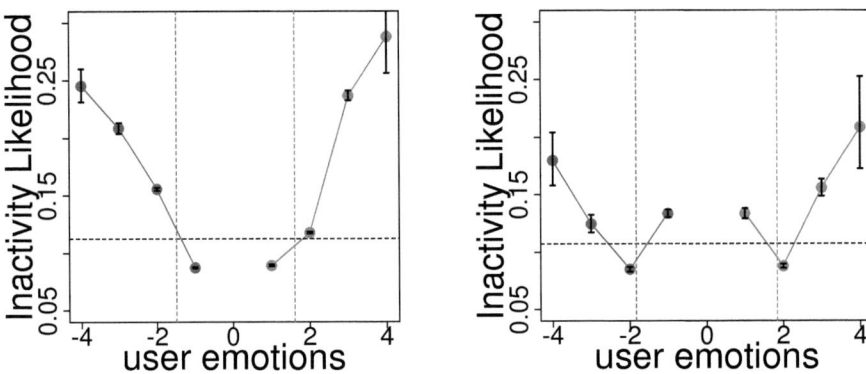

**Figure 4.5:** Likelihood of an interval to be labeled as *INA* given contributor emotions, $P(I = \text{INA}|N_u)$ (red) and $P(I = \text{INA}|P_u)$ (green), for the bug tracker (left) and the mailing list (right). Error bars show confidence intervals, the horizontal dashed lines indicate $P(I = \text{INA})$ and vertical bars the means of $N_u$ and $P_u$ in each dataset.

The distinctive v-shape of the likelihood for the emotions in the mailing list (Figure 4.5 right) implies that lack of emotions can also serve as an indicator for contributors becoming inactive, but only when shared with others through the mailing list. It is remarkable that both $N_u$ and $P_u$ are informative to discriminate periods of inactivity in both datasets, suggesting that the decision to become inactive is more related to emotional intensity in general, rather than to positive or negative emotions alone. This is in line with the psychological theory which states that certain levels of arousal, or emotion intensity, are motivators for activity [186].

### 4.5.4 Real-time prediction

We apply the Bayesian analysis explained above to predict when contributors are going to start periods of inactivity, solely based on the emotional content of their messages. Given

## 4.5. EMOTIONS AND INACTIVITY

the results shown in Figure 4.5, we apply two different models:

1. bug tracker: if $|N_u| > \Theta_1$ or $|P_u| > \Theta_1$, then the next interval is predicted to be *INA*, and *ACT* otherwise.

2. mailing list: if $|N_u - \bar{N}_u| > \Theta_2$ or $|P_u - \bar{P}_u| > \Theta_2$, then the next interval is predicted to be *INA*, and *ACT* otherwise, where $\bar{N}_u$ and $\bar{P}_u$ are the average values of emotions expressed by this contributor.

We apply the above predictors with $\Theta_1 = 1.9$ and $\Theta_2 = 0.8$ (thresholds corresponding to a tradeoff between *precision* and *recall*, favoring *recall*) to each point in our datasets, and compute values of *precision* and *recall* [110] over 20 bootstrapped samples, to ensure the robustness of our predictor. Table 4.4 reports the means and standard deviations of *precision* and *recall* for each class and dataset. Both predictors have *precision* significantly higher than the *prior* probabilities in the respective classes. In particular, the *precision* of the minority class, *INA*, is sufficiently above the *prior* probability $P(I = \text{INA})$, showing that our method produce meaningful results when using contributor emotions to predict when these are at risk of becoming inactive. In addition, the values of *recall* for both classes are well above 0.6, correctly classifying most of the existing instances.

**Table 4.4:** Results of the prediction of contributors becoming inactive or remaining active in both datasets. Standard deviations of *precision* and *recall* values are calculated over 20 bootstrapped samples of the datasets. The row *prior* refers to the prior probability of *Active* and *Inactive* found in our sample.

|           | GENTOO BUGZILLA | |
|-----------|-----------------|------------------|
| measure   | Active          | Inactive         |
| prior     | $0.886 \pm 0.030$ | $0.112 \pm 0.030$ |
| precision | $0.930 \pm 0.024$ | $0.196 \pm 0.019$ |
| recall    | $0.673 \pm 0.087$ | $0.624 \pm 0.012$ |

|           | GENTOO-DEV | |
|-----------|------------|------------------|
| measure   | Active     | Inactive         |
| prior     | $0.892 \pm 0.032$ | $0.107 \pm 0.032$ |
| precision | $0.931 \pm 0.026$ | $0.175 \pm 0.030$ |
| recall    | $0.654 \pm 0.072$ | $0.623 \pm 0.021$ |

## 4.6 Threats to Validity

In our analysis, we do not consider the hierarchical organization of messages ("reply to" structure), neither their time dynamics. Even with this limited approach, our methods provide insightful results, especially for their quantitative explanatory power with regards to *Alice*'s justification on her departure. We argue that future research should focus on the dynamics of emotions and investigate if there are underlining preferential paths [164].

## 4.7 Conclusion

Based on a case study of the GENTOO project (see Chapter 3), we analyze the relation between emotions and activity of its contributors. We gather two disjoint datasets of communication within the community: (i) the bug reports stored in its bug tracking system BUGZILLA, and (ii) the messages posted in the developer's mailing list. We provide a sentiment analysis of the messages written by all the contributors and relate the emotional expressions to the activity patterns.

The first part of our case study investigates the emotional components related to the leave of a central contributor, named *Alice*. We show that her email discussions with other contributors were more negative than the rest, and that her departure was followed by higher stages of negativity in the community during its reorganization.

We extend this analysis to contributors in general, both in the bug tracker and the mailing list. To detect inactivity, we apply current *state of the art* theories on human correlated behavior, finding a mode of interevent times that indicates stages of contributor inactivity. This allows us to statistically analyze the relation between a contributor's emotional expressions and its individual intervals of inactivity. We reveal preconditions of emotional expressions that indicate when contributors feel demotivated to further contribute to the project. Based on this, we are able to estimate when a contributor becomes inactive, based on emotions expressed on his last messages. With this, we provide a tractable approach that can be applied by community managers to monitor emotional interaction within the community, and to foster timely reaction against undesirable turnover events of contributors.

Our contributions do not only focus on predictive results, but provide additional insights into the phenomenon at hand, in particular into fundamental relations between emotions and activity (and implicitly into motivation). We find that it is the emotional *intensity* which defines activity, rather than its *polarity*. Thus, in this work, we took a step for-

## 4.7. CONCLUSION 85

ward by providing a methodology based on *sentiment* analysis, which sheds new light on GENTOO's case study. This unveils a wide horizon of new quantitative approaches to the analysis of social dynamics within online communities, extending previous approaches to online emotional interaction [78], and social resilience [81].

# Chapter 5

# Triaging Bugs with Social Networks

### Summary

Based on the methodology presented in chapters 2 and 3, we propose an accurate and practical approach to automatize bug report triaging. We demonstrate its relevance and applicability in a case study, using a comprehensive data set of more than 700, 000 bug reports–corresponding to a period of more than ten years–obtained from the bug tracking records of four major OSS communities. We observe that the centrality of contributors–embedded in the social network largest connected component–is a strong indicator for the final resolution category (or quality) of their bug reports. More specifically, the higher the centrality of contributors, the higher the likelihood that their bug reports will be fixed improving the software. Based on this finding, we apply machine learning to identify valid bug reports at reporting time. Among the four case studies considered here, we observe precision ranging from 78.9% to 90.3%, while the recall range is from 38.9% to 91.0%. The literature on automated bug report triaging offers no match to our high accuracy results solely based on social network analysis.

## 5.1 Introduction

Triaging and processing bug reports is an important task in collaborative software engineering and it can crucially affect product quality, project reputation, contributor motivation and thus the long-term success of a project. Practical experience from large OSS projects confirms that–particularly in projects with large numbers of comparably inexperienced part-time contributors–the process of triaging, categorizing and prioritizing bug reports can become a laborious and difficult task, consuming considerable resources (see [90], e.g. fact 31). Both the importance and complexity of this problem can be illustrated by a simple example: out of the more than $64,000$ bug reports that have been resolved by the community of the MOZILLA FIREFOX project, more than $50,000$ (or $\approx 78\%$) of these reports have eventually been identified either as *duplicates* of known bugs, *invalid* reports that refer to misunderstanding rather than a software issue or *incomplete* reports which lack basic information required to reproduce the alleged bug. The magnitude of this problem in large-scale projects calls for (semi-)automated techniques that assist bug handling communities in the triaging and prioritization of bug reports. The provision of methods which are able to automatically identify *valid* bug reports with high precision and recall can have huge implications for practitioners of collaborative and distributed software engineering: being able to filter, assign and prioritize those bug reports that likely result in a bug fix can significantly improve the responsiveness of support communities. Furthermore, a temporary deferral of those bug reports that are likely to be duplicates, invalid or incomplete to a moderation queue can considerably alleviate the effort required for bug triaging. It can also be used to automatically enforce the adherence to community guidelines, e.g. by automatically asking original reporters to reconfirm that reported bugs are neither duplicates nor incomplete.

Due to the importance for practical software engineering, a number of different approaches for the automated classification of bug reports have been studied, among them approaches based on the automated assessment of information provided by bug reports [10, 26, 110, 193], natural language processing [51, 176, 221], the temporal dynamics of bug handling processes [166], coordination patterns [36], or the reputation of bug reporters [96, 236, 246]. Based on a unique data set containing the full history of more than $700,000$ bug reports in four major OSS communities, in this chapter we consider to what extent automated bug classification techniques can be based on *quantitative measures for the social embeddedness of bug reporters in the project's community*. We particularly address this question from the perspective of complex, evolving collaboration networks and the computation of node-centric metrics that capture structural properties like centrality and clustering.

Our contributions to the current state of research are the following:

- We study relations between the centrality of bug reporters and the eventual outcome of the bug triaging process. For the four OSS communities studied in this chapter, we find strong evidence for the hypothesis that the centrality of bug reporters in the collaboration network is indicative for the quality of bug reports.

- We show that quantitative measures for the bug reporter's position in the collaboration network can be used for an automated classification of valid bug reports. For the four studied OSS communities, we find that this classification achieves precision ranging from 78.9% to 90.3%, while the recall range is from 38.9% to 91.0%.

With this, we extend previous works that have studied automated classification of bugs that are eventually fixed. In particular, we use a more comprehensive data set, more sophisticated quantitative measures for bug reporter's position in the evolving structures of a community as well as a predictive modeling approach that is based on a support vector machine. In the following section, we provide a more detailed review of existing literature on automated bug classification and prediction mechanisms as well social aspects of collaborative software engineering. From this we then extract a set of open research questions that are addressed in the remaining sections of this chapter.

## 5.2 Social Aspects in Bug Report Processing

The distribution of contributions, the structure and evolution of collaboration networks in OSS projects, as well as their relation with individual and collective performance have been studied in a number of works. A quantitative study of the development efforts in the projects APACHE and MOZILLA has been presented in [147]. Among other aspects, the distribution of contributions across community members has been analyzed. For the APACHE project, the authors particularly validate that–while coding efforts are mainly concentrated on a small set of core developers–the bug handling and reporting process is based on a much larger community of part-time contributors.

Apart from the mere distribution of contributions, the topology of communication and collaborations between contributors is an interesting field of study. The relation between the network position of developers in bug handling communities and their success rate (in terms of the number of bugs the developers fix) has been studied in [65]. There, the authors find that developers with higher node degree fix bugs at a higher rate. Furthermore, the authors provide implications for future research, calling for subsequent studies

## 5.2. SOCIAL ASPECTS IN BUG REPORT PROCESSING

of the relation between communication structures and individual as well as team-based performance. Our work complements the study of [65] in the sense that we investigate the relation between the centrality of bug reporters and their individual performance, i.e. whether the reports are eventually found to refer to actual software issues. Our methods are based on earlier work quantifying the dynamics of social organization in OSS communities [239]. Social mechanisms underlying the impact of communication topologies on bug handling performance have been studied in [23]. There, the authors conclude that the most difficult task of successfully handling bugs is the mediation between the users and the developers of a project. Similar results have been presented by the authors of [220], whose analysis is based on the bug handling communities of two major OSS projects. Their analysis verifies that the collaborative identification of the cause of a software defect is one of the most difficult tasks that needs to be solved before bugs can be properly addressed by developers. Based on data obtained from the bug handling community of the ECLIPSE project and similar to our approach, in [21] measures of communication dynamics and user centrality have been studied in networks constructed based on user comments and $CC$ subscriptions. The findings suggest that the centrality of users in the communication flow networks extracted from BUGZILLA data is related to the future failure proneness of code. Similarly, the relationship between communication structures and success at the collective level has been studied in [230] and [229]. In those papers, the use of social network structures and communication deficiencies for the prediction of build failures has been proposed. Furthermore, it was found that positive team performance is related to communication structures that facilitate information dissemination. These quantitative insights about the social dimension of software engineering highlight the importance of social indicators and provide an important foundation for our approach of using related measures from social network analysis for the classification of bug report quality.

Due to the difficulty of handling user contributed bug reports in large-scale projects with millions of users, a number of different approaches for supporting bug triaging processes based on an automatic classification of bug reports have been studied. In [110] a simple linear regression model for the quality of bug reports has been proposed based on a data set of 27,984 bug reports from the project MOZILLA FIREFOX. The model is based both on information available at the time of submission as well as post-submission data like the number of comments or attachments added during the first hours and days. The evaluation of a model based on this data shows that there is a 5% increase of predictive power compared to a pure chance prediction. In a case study on the ECLIPSE project [193], a predictive model has been introduced that is based on the textual information in comments and the bug description. The analysis shows that the model yields a precision of 62.9% and a recall of 84.5% when predicting which bugs will be reopened after being marked as closed. Apart from simple regression models, machine learning approaches have been used for the automated classification and triaging of bug reports in a number of works [10, 26, 59, 166, 196]. In [10], the use of machine learning techniques for assisting humans in assigning bugs to developers has been proposed. In [26] a machine learning approach is used to reduce bug tossing, i.e. the simultaneous assignment of bugs to multiple developers. The authors show that bug tossing can be reduced significantly when classifying developers according to the product relationships of previously fixed bugs. In [196] different machine learning approaches have been applied to bug descriptions and comments stored in the BUGZILLA database of the ECLIPSE project. Here the authors prove the suitability of support vector machines and Latent Dirichlet Allocations for the prediction of the category of bug reports.

Indicators for the *social context* of users have been considered for the prediction of which bugs get fixed and which are likely to be reopened in [96, 246]. In [96], a number of bug report features have been used, including the reputation of bug reporters in terms of the fraction of their previously reported bugs that were eventually fixed. The authors show that a statistical model for the automated identification of those bugs that will get fixed can yield a precision of 68% and a recall of 64%. The same approach has recently shown to be successful for the prediction of which bugs get reopened [246].

Data from the BUGZILLA installations of ECLIPSE and MOZILLA have been used in [236] to model developer prioritization in bug repositories. Here the authors used a ranking of developers based on social networks and apply a support vector machine to predict the severity of bug reports assigned to developers. In [25], a predictive model for the bug severity based on the location of the defect in the software dependency network has been studied. Here the authors find that the degree of components in the software is indicative for the severity of bugs.

## 5.3 Study Design and Methodology

Based on a review of existing work that is related to a) the influence of social embeddedness on the performance of communities and individual contributors and b) the automated classification of bug reports, we identify the following open research questions which will be addressed in this chapter:

**RQ1** *Is the position of bug reporters in the evolving collaboration structures of bug handling communities related to the quality of contributed bug reports?*

## 5.3. STUDY DESIGN AND METHODOLOGY 91

**RQ2** *Can quantitative measures for the position of bug reporters be used to predict which bug reports refer to valid bugs?*

With the prediction methodology proposed in section 5.5, we extend and improve previous approaches to automated bug classification in a number of ways: First we consider a larger data set which contains a total of more than 5.8 million time-stamped change events for more than 700, 000 bug reports from four large OSS projects. Second, rather than using simple, one-dimensional social indicators like the number of previously submitted reports or the number of connections, we use a set of nine topological measures to quantify the position of bug reporters in the collaboration network, among them a comprehensive set of centrality measures as well as degree, local clustering structure and membership in the largest network component. Third, rather than taking a simple static perspective, we consider *evolving collaboration networks* by using fine-grained temporal data on collaboration and communication events. Based on these features, we apply a machine learning approach for predicting which of the bug reports are eventually identified as valid, i.e. which are referring to actual bugs that need to be addressed by the community. We further strictly limit our prediction methodology to *only include information available at the time of the submission of a bug report, thus making the approach directly applicable in a practical setting*. To the best of our knowledge, no prior work has combined such a comprehensive set of network measures on evolving networks with a machine learning classifier and applied it to data set of similar scale. Our findings show that our methods significantly improve the precision and recall of existing automated bug classification schemes.

In this chapter, we adopt a data-driven approach that is based on a data set we collected from the MOZILLA BUGZILLA[191] installations of the four communities evolving around the following OSS projects: MOZILLA FIREFOX, MOZILLA THUNDERBIRD, ECLIPSE and NETBEANS. In the following, we provide a detailed description of a) the data retrieval process and the categories of bug reports available in the data, b) our methodology of extracting time-stamped collaboration networks and c) the measures applied in our analysis.

### 5.3.1 Data Retrieval

Records retrievable via the BUGZILLA *API* are centered around *bug reports* which are identified by a unique *bug Id*. Further, contributors registered in the BUGZILLA installation of the respective OSS project are also identified by their unique *contributor Id*. Each bug report has a number of associated fields, for which the history of all updates along with a time stamp and the *Id* of the contributor who has changed the field, is stored in the database. For our analysis, we use the *contributor Id* of the contributor who initially

**Table 5.1:** Time periods, number of bugs, number of change events and number of bugs with particular status. The different bug resolution categories are the following: *FIX* for fixed, *DUP* for duplicate, *INV* for invalid, *WOF* for won't fix and finally *INC* for incomplete. More details in section 5.3.1.

|  | FIREFOX | THUNDERBIRD | ECLIPSE | NETBEANS | Total |
|---|---|---|---|---|---|
| Start date | April 2002 | January 2000 | October 2001 | January 1999 | – |
| Total bug reports | 112,968 | 35,388 | 356,415 | 210,921 | 715,692 |
| Change events | 1,068,070 | 313,957 | 2,594,385 | 1,875,878 | 5,852,290 |
| Changes / report | 9.45 | 8.87 | 7.28 | 8.89 | 8.18 |
| Resolved bugs (resolved/total) | 64,088 (0.57) | 21,644 (0.61) | 158,957 (0.45) | 42,851 (0.19) | 287,540 (0.40) |
| FIX (FIX / resolved) | 10,856 (0.17) | 4,508 (0.21) | 103,453 (0.65) | 21,442 (0.50) | 140,259 (0.49) |
| DUP (DUP / resolved) | 24,263 (0.38) | 10,336 (0.48) | 28,227 (0.18) | 9,328 (0.22) | 72,154 (0.25) |
| INV (INV /resolved) | 11,785 (0.18) | 2,829 (0.13) | 12,601 (0.08) | 4,082 (0.10) | 31,297 (0.11) |
| WOF (WOF / resolved) | 2,708 (0.04) | 581 (0.03) | 14,676 (0.09) | 5,515 (0.13) | 23,480 (0.08) |
| INC (INC / resolved) | 14,476 (0.23) | 3,390 (0.16) | - | 2484 (0.06) | 20,350 (0.07) |

submitted the bug report (throughout the chapter we will refer to this contributor as the *bug reporter*), the time stamp of the initial submission, and the status of the bug report (e.g. *unconfirmed, pending, reproduced, resolved*). We further use the *contributor Id* of the so-called *ASSIGNEE*, who is a contributor responsible for providing a fix to the bug, and a list of *contributor Id's* of those contributors that have (or were) subscribed to receive subsequent updates on the bug report, *CC*.

For our study, we retrieved the full history of all bug reports via the *API* of the respective projects. Our data set contains roughly 715,000 bug reports and 5.8 Million change events recorded in the time between January 1999 and June 2012. Table 5.1 presents some basic statistics of the data set used throughout this chapter.

In particular, our analysis is focused on a subset of those 287,540 bug reports that had a final status indicating that they were *resolved*. We limit our analysis to these bug reports because the bug handling community already completed the triaging process and thus reached a decision on how they were processed. For this subset of resolved bugs we extract the full history of change events and categorize each bug according to the final change in the *Resolution* field of the corresponding record. Bugs that had a final *Resolution* status of *FIXED* (i.e. an issue that is fixed improving the software), *INVALID* (i.e. the report refers to misconception w.r.t. the expected behavior or wrong usage rather than to a software bug), *DUPLICATE* (i.e. the report refers to a bug that has already been reported) or *WONTFIX* (i.e. the bug is valid and reproducible but it will not be fixed due to a lack of resources or low priority) were categorized accordingly. In addition, we consider a bug report to fall into the category *INCOMPLETE* whenever it had an intermediate status that indicates that the initial bug report was missing information required to properly triage the bug. While the projects MOZILLA FIREFOX, MOZILLA THUNDERBIRD and NETBEANS make use of a specific status for incomplete reports, in the ECLIPSE community, bug reports that lack necessary information simply remain in the initial status *NEW*. Since this procedure does not allow us to easily classify corresponding bugs, we disregard the *INCOMPLETE* category for the ECLIPSE project.

### 5.3.2 Network Construction

Our approach to utilize measures for the embeddedness of bug reporters in the community is based on the extraction of social networks. Those can be viewed as proxies for the collaboration and communication structure of an OSS project during a particular period of time. Our data set is comprehensive in that it contains a history of all events associated with all bugs reported during a period of more than ten years. For the construction of social networks we focus on those update events that directly capture dyadic interactions, and therefore can arguably be interpreted as pairwise interactions between contributors. In particular, we use the dyadic relations *ASSIGN* and *CC* for this purpose. For the present study, we decided to neglect additionally available information like the sequence of comments on bugs for which the inference of direct interactions between contributors is more difficult and necessarily error-prone. Any contributor can add *contributor IDs* to the *CC* list of a bug report, which will make sure that the added contributor receives information on all future updated of a particular bug. Special permissions are required for a contributor to *ASSIGN* a bug to another contributor, which is hence being made responsible for providing a solution for the issue. We would like to emphasise that focusing on *CC* and *ASSIGN* updates necessarily provides a limited perspective on the interactions between contributors. Nevertheless we argue that the generated social networks are insightful with respect to the collaboration and communication structures of a project: A *CC* interaction between contributors $A$ and $B$ indicates that $A$ is aware of $B$ and that $A$ knows what $B$ is interested in. In addition, an *ASSIGN* interaction between $A$ and $B$ is indicative for different roles in the community. For example, contributor $A$ identifies the cause of a bug and assigns it to contributor $B$ who is a developer and likely able to fix it.

The simplest, and usually adopted, approach to analyze social networks in OSS communities is to study the topology by aggregating all interactions throughout the history of a project. However, since our data set covers interactions from more than one decade, the meaningfulness of such aggregated structures is questionable. It is likely that most of the contributors represented by nodes in the aggregated network never have been active within the same time period. This clearly limits the expressiveness of the network structure in terms of a project's "social organization". In order to overcome this shortcoming, we make use of the fact that–like all other updates in our data set–*CC* and *ASSIGN* interactions have a precise time stamp. In our analysis, we particularly study networks of collaborations constructed by aggregating all interactions occurring within time windows with a length of 30 days. This allows us to focus on collaboration networks existing at short periods of time during the project's history, e.g. when particular contributors were present, particular bugs were reported or when the project had a particular level of popularity and maturity. In the following, we provide a detailed description of the quantitative measures used in our analysis of the resulting time-stamped collaboration networks.

### 5.3.3 Network Measures

We adopt (social) network measures to capture the social organization in bug handling communities [152, 222] (see also chapters 2 and 3).

**Centrality measures**

Node-centric measures of *centrality* allow us to assess the relative *importance* of nodes in a given network. This importance, or centrality, can be expressed through different approaches. The simplest one is the number of connections a node has to other nodes, known as the *degree centrality*. In a social context, degree centrality can be interpreted either in terms of the potential impact of a node on other nodes or as the amount of information available to a node. However, degree centrality does not capture the actual *position* of a node in the network in terms of how close a node is to *all* other nodes. A further important measure is thus the so-called *closeness centrality* [75], which is defined as the inverse of the sum of all distances to all other nodes. The centrality of nodes can be also measured in terms of the role they play in connecting other nodes. The so-called *betweenness centrality* is given by the total number of shortest paths between all possible pairs of nodes that pass through a node [222].

*Eigenvector centrality* is a more sophisticated feedback centrality measure in which the centrality of a node is recursively influenced by the centrality of its direct neighbors:

$$Ev(n_i) = \frac{1}{\lambda} \sum_{n_j \in M(n_i)} Ev(n_j)$$

Here $M(n_i)$ is the set of direct neighbors of node $n_i$ and $\lambda$ is the largest eigenvalue of the network's adjacency matrix $A$ [152]. In other words, nodes connected to highly central nodes increase their own centrality. For our analysis, we use the eigenvector centrality implementation of the IGRAPH library [50] for the R language [168]. The last two measures considered are the *clustering coefficient* and *k-coreness*. The first captures to what degree two nodes that have a neighbor in common are also neighbors. The second one is based on a network decomposition such that nodes are assigned to so-called *shells* of the network topology. Nodes belong to a given shell $k$ if they have a degree $k$ after removing all other nodes with degree up to $k-1$. Nodes in shells with higher number can be seen to have higher relative influence within a community [79].

**Analysis of Largest Connected Component**

In large-scale, sparse social networks usually not all nodes have a link to the rest of the network, i.e. some parts can be isolated. Thus, in addition to connected parts (components) of the network, a number of disconnected components exist. Several network measures, including eigenvector centrality, are not well defined for networks with different connected components. To overcome this problem, we restrict our analysis to the so-called *largest connected component* (LCC) of the monthly collaboration networks. We find that the fraction of nodes in the LCC was high: For ECLIPSE, an average fraction of 0.78 of all contributors in the monthly collaboration network belong to the LCC, for NETBEANS the average fraction is 0.96, for MOZILLA THUNDERBIRD 0.53 and for MOZILLA FIREFOX 0.58. Moreover, we verified that the largest size of the remaining components was insignificant when compared to the size of the LCC. To illustrate our approach, in Figure 5.1 we show the components of a monthly collaboration network for each of the four projects studied in our analysis. In each of these networks of comparable size the LCC is highlighted. Structural differences between these networks indicate significant variations in the social organization of the four projects.

## 5.4 User Centrality and Bug Report Quality

In this section we apply the methods introduced in section 5.3 to address research question **RQ1**. From a network perspective, this question can be rewritten in the following way:

*Is the centrality of bug reporters in the collaboration network related to the quality of the submitted bug reports?*

A positive answer to this question could serve as a foundation for the development of automated bug classification schemes that are based on methods from social network analysis. We investigate this question for four major OSS projects that adopt the BUGZILLA bug tracking system: ECLIPSE, NETBEANS, MOZILLA FIREFOX and MOZILLA THUNDERBIRD. Using the data set described in section 5.3.1, we analyze the history of all bugs that were eventually marked as *resolved*, along with the corresponding resolution categories.

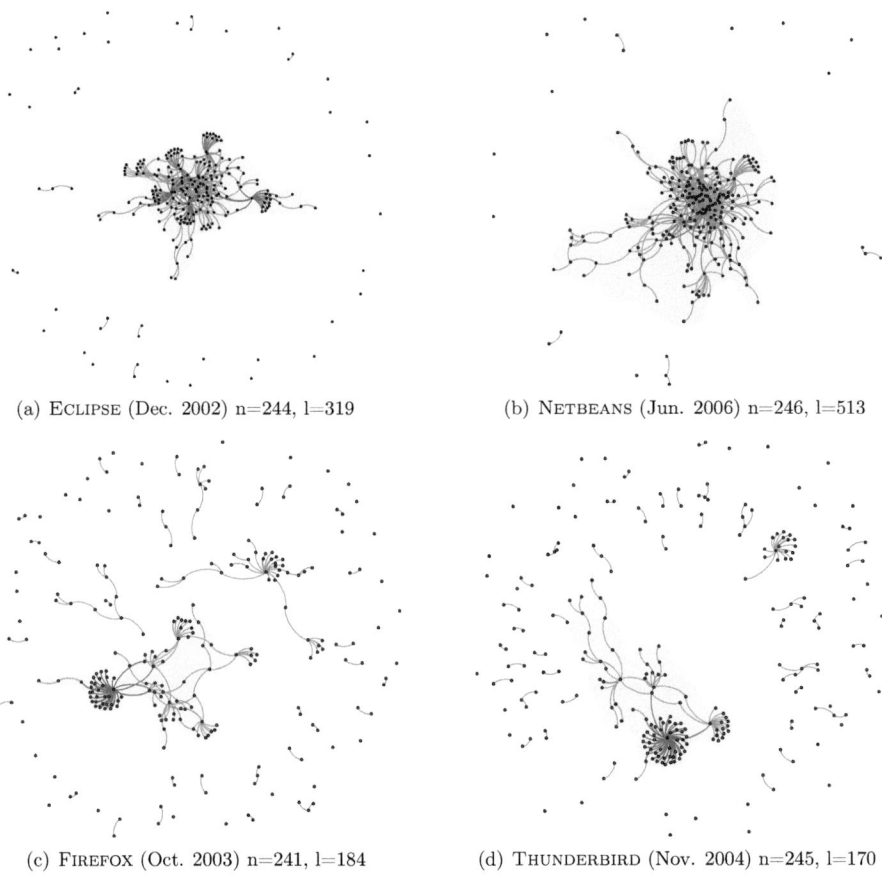

**Figure 5.1:** Four monthly collaboration networks representing the communities of ECLIPSE, NETBEANS, FIREFOX and THUNDERBIRD. Although the networks are of similar size (i.e. in terms of nodes $n$ and links $l$), the different topological structures indicate that these communities differ largely in terms of social organization. The yellow shaded area represents the network's largest connected component (LCC).

As emphasized before, the *resolved* bugs are the ones for which the bug report processing was completed (see section 5.3.1 for details). The resolution categories are: *FIXED*, *DUPLICATE*, *INVALID*, *WONTFIX* and *INCOMPLETE*. In addition, we consider bugs to fall in the category *INCOMPLETE*, if a bug report had this status at some point in

## 5.4. USER CENTRALITY AND BUG REPORT QUALITY

its history, independently of the final resolution category. According to the bug handling guidelines of the respective communities, bug reports will only be marked as such if the reporter failed to include the required additional information within a certain period of time. Some basic statistics about the total and relative number of bugs falling in the different categories are given in Table 5.1.

In line with our research question, we first hypothesize that the submission of "helpful" bug reports–those that eventually result in a bug fix–increases the centrality of the bug reporter, i.e.

**H1:** *The centrality of bug reporters increase after the submission of bug reports that eventually result in a bug fix.*

Complementary to **H1** we can furthermore hypothesize:

**H2:** *The centrality of bug reporters decrease after the submission of bug reports that are eventually identified as duplicate or invalid.*

While these two hypotheses address the relation between the submission of helpful or duplicate bug reports and *subsequent changes* of the bug reporters' centrality in the community, it is also reasonable to consider an inverse dependence: The bug reporters' centrality at the time when a bug is reported can possibly influence their ability to contribute helpful bug reports. A better knowledge of bug handling procedures that results from a higher centrality in the community may for instance help to prevent duplicate bug reports. In our third hypothesis–which is also the basis for our prediction method–we thus propose that the centrality of bug reporters is indicative for the outcome of the bug handling process.

**H3:** *The centrality of a bug reporter in the monthly collaboration network preceding the time of the report is indicative for the eventual outcome of the bug handling process.*

We would like to emphasize that one can imagine different mechanisms, both at the level of the bug reporter and the community that are compatible with these hypotheses. As mentioned above, the bug reporters' centrality in the network is likely to be correlated with the level of contribution as well as the knowledge and experience of contributors. These factors are likely to influence the quality of bug reports submitted by a contributor. Furthermore, being central in the community can influence the attention received by other contributors, thus increasing the chance of bug reports being taken seriously, prioritized and eventually fixed.

**Table 5.2:** Comparison of eigenvector centrality distributions for the five bug resolution categories considered in our analysis. In each row we present the hypothesis being tested, the corresponding distributions involved (e.g. $FIX_1 \sim FIX_2$), the alternative hypothesis (i.e. $>,<,\neq$), its respective $p$-value (we indicate with (*) when we accept the alternative hypothesis) and the sample size of each distribution (i.e. number of bugs). More details in section 5.4.1.

| Hypothesis | Comparison of Distrib. | FIREFOX | THUNDERBIRD | ECLIPSE | NETBEANS |
|---|---|---|---|---|---|
| H1 | $FIX_1 \sim FIX_2$ | $<, p = 0.0026$, (*) (5847, 6140) | $>, p = 0.0351$, (*) (2139, 2377) | $\neq, p = 0.1453$ (66208, 69026) | $\neq, p = 0.6435$ (13930, 14668) |
| H2 | $DUP_1 \sim DUP_2$ | $>, p = 0.0349$, (*) (6799, 8697) | $>, p < 2.22e-16$, (*) (973, 3027) | $>, p < 2.22e-16$, (*) (17600, 22215) | $>, p < 2.22e-16$, (*) (3984, 5470) |
| H2 | $INV_1 \sim INV_2$ | $\neq, p = 0.7268$ (1321, 1394) | $>, p = 0.0449$, (*) (242, 297) | $\neq, p = 0.8489$ (5313, 5958) | $\neq, p = 0.1266$ (1906, 2066) |
| H3 | $FIX_1 \sim WOF_1$ | $>, p = 1.81e-10$, (*) (5847, 1022) | $>, p = 1.58e-06$, (*) (2139, 106) | $<, p < 2.22e-16$, (*) (66208, 7769) | $>, p < 2.22e-16$, (*) (13930, 2847) |
| H3 | $FIX_1 \sim DUP_1$ | $>, p < 2.22e-16$, (*) (5847, 6799) | $>, p < 2.22e-16$, (*) (2139, 973) | $<, p < 2.22e-16$, (*) (66208, 17600) | $>, p < 2.22e-16$, (*) (13930, 3984) |
| H3 | $FIX_1 \sim INV_1$ | $>, p < 2.22e-16$, (*) (5847, 1321) | $>, p = 4.93e-10$, (*) (2139, 242) | $<, p < 2.22e-16$, (*) (66208, 5313) | $>, p < 2.22e-16$, (*) (13930, 1906) |
| H3 | $FIX_1 \sim INC_1$ | $>, p < 2.22e-16$, (*) (5847, 587) | $>, p < 2.22e-16$, (*) (2139, 159) | (-)(-) (66208, 0) | $>, p < 2.22e-16$, (*) (13930, 661) |

## 5.4.1 Analysis

We test hypotheses **H1**, **H2** and **H3** in the following way: We first categorize all bug reports that were eventually resolved according to their final resolution. As described in section 5.3.2, we then extract the collaboration networks in the month preceding and following the time of the bug report and compute the eigenvector centrality of bug reporters in both networks. By this, we obtain five distributions of centralities of bug reporters in the monthly collaboration network *preceding* the time of the bug report for the bug categories *FIXED, DUPLICATE, INVALID, WONTFIX* and *INCOMPLETE*. We denote these as $FIX_1$, $DUP_1$, $INV_1$, $WOF_1$ and $INC_1$ respectively. Similarly, we extract the distributions of eigenvector centralities of bug reporters in the month *after* the bug report and denote these as $FIX_2$, $DUP_2$, $INV_2$, $WOF_2$ and $INC_2$. We would like to emphasize that–out of the quantitative measures introduced in section 5.3.3–in this section we only use eigenvector centrality to quantify the position of bug reporters. We focus on this particular measure for it expresses the centrality of a contributor as a function of its degree and the centrality of its direct neighbors (see Figure 1.6 in Chapter 1). Thus, we can capture direct and indirect *knowledge spillovers* with a single measure [70] . However, for the classifier proposed in the next section we use a more comprehensive set consisting of additional topological measures for centrality, coreness, degree and membership in the LCC.

In order to compare the eigenvector centrality distributions of bug reporters, according to the resolution categories described above, we apply a *Wilcoxon-Mann-Whitney* test [109]. For two samples $S_A$ and $S_B$ drawn from two distributions $F_A$ and $F_B$ with $F_A(x) = F_B(x - \alpha)$, the *Wilcoxon-Mann-Whitney* infers the stochastic ordering of the distributions, i.e. whether the shift parameter $\alpha$ is likely to be larger than zero (i.e. $F_A > F_B$) or smaller than zero (i.e. $F_A < F_B$). Based on the null hypothesis that $\alpha = 0$ (i.e. $F_A \sim F_B$) the test is executed either with the one-sided alternative hypotheses $F_A > F_B$ or $F_A < F_B$, or with a two-sided alternative hypothesis $F_A \neq F_B$. For each of the three alternative hypotheses, the test yields a *p*-value which–if it is below a given significance threshold–is used to reject the null hypothesis in favor of the alternative hypothesis. If none of the *p*-values for one of the alternative hypotheses is below the significance threshold, one cannot reject the *null hypothesis* that both samples $S_A$ and $S_B$ are in fact drawn from the same distribution, i.e. $F_A \sim F_B$.

We now test **H1** by applying the methodology described above to the two samples $FIX_1$ and $FIX_2$, i.e. we test whether there is an increase in the eigenvector centralities of bug reporters after the report of a bug that is eventually fixed. The null hypothesis **H0** related to **H1** is that the samples $FIX_1$ and $FIX_2$ are drawn from the *same distribution*, i.e. $FIX_1 \sim FIX_2$ or–in other words–the eigenvector centrality of a reporter of helpful bugs *does not change* after the time of the report. We reject the null hypothesis and accept hypothesis **H1** if the $p$-value for $FIX_1 < FIX_2$ is below a significance threshold of 0.05. The resulting $p$-values for the comparison of the distributions $FIX_1$ and $FIX_2$ are given in Table 5.2. We can observe that for the projects ECLIPSE and NETBEANS one cannot reject the null hypothesis that eigenvector centralities of bug reporters *do not change* after the submission of bug reports that result in a bug fix. However, for MOZILLA FIREFOX *there is a significant increase* in the eigenvector centralities of bug reporters reporting bugs that are eventually fixed. Interestingly, for MOZILLA THUNDERBIRD *we also reject the null hypothesis but instead find a significant decrease of eigenvector centrality*.

Similar to **H1**, we test hypothesis **H2** by applying a *Wilcoxon-Mann-Whitney* test on the samples $DUP_1$, $INV_1$, $DUP_2$ and $INV_2$, i.e. we compare the eigenvector centrality distributions of bug reporters submitting duplicate or invalid bug reports *before* and *after* the time of the submission. The results shown in Table 5.2 provide strong evidence for hypothesis **H2** regarding bugs that are eventually identified as duplicates. In fact, the null hypothesis that $DUP_1$ and $DUP_2$ are drawn from the same distribution can be rejected in favor of the alternative hypothesis $DUP_1 > DUP_2$ for all of the studied projects. For the case of bugs that are eventually identified as *invalid*, we cannot reject the null hypothesis for the projects FIREFOX, ECLIPSE and NETBEANS. For the project THUNDERBIRD the null hypothesis can be rejected in favor of hypothesis **H2**.

Finally, we test hypothesis **H3** by comparing the distribution $FIX_1$ to the distributions $WOF_1$, $DUP_1$, $INV_1$ and $INC_1$, i.e. we check whether the centralities of reporters of bugs that are eventually fixed are–on average–different than of those reporting bugs that fall in other categories. The results of our analysis are shown in Table 5.2. We find strong evidence for hypothesis **H3** when comparing $FIX_1$ to either $WOF_1$, $DUP_1$, $INV_1$ or $INC_1$. In the projects FIREFOX, THUNDERBIRD and NETBEANS we particularly find that the centrality of reporters of bugs that are eventually fixed is significantly larger. Interestingly, the opposite relation holds for the project *Eclipse*, i.e. here the centrality of reporters of bugs that are eventually fixed is significantly smaller.

In summary, our analysis validates that there is a statistically significant relation between the centrality of a bug reporter and the outcome of bug handling processes. We particularly emphasize that our analysis supports **H3**: the hypothesis that the centrality in the collaboration network during the month preceding the bug report is indicative for the outcome of the bug handling process. In the following section, we make use of this finding to develop a prediction method that can e.g. be applied in (semi-)automatic bug report prioritization strategies. By this, we show that a quantitative analysis of social structures in OSS communities can assist in bug triaging. While in the next section we exclusively focus on the use of a set measures of *social embeddedness*, we would like to highlight that a combination of these measures with existing methods is likely to further improve the classification mechanism.

## 5.5 Classification of Bugs with Social Networks

Based on the observed relations between the bug reporters' centrality and bug report quality presented in section 5.4, we now address research question **RQ2**, specifically:

*Can quantitative measures for the position of bug reporters be used to predict which bug reports refer to valid bugs?*

The goal is to develop a practical method that makes use of topological measures for the position of bug reporters in the collaboration network. In order to facilitate the bug triaging process, we particularly aim at predicting whether a bug report is likely to be either *Valid* or *Faulty*. As *Valid* bug reports, we consider all bug reports that have a final status of *FIXED* or *WONTFIX*[1]. Conversely–and in line with the semantics of bug categories provided in section 5.3.1–we consider all bug reports as *Faulty* that have a final status of *DUPLICATE, INVALID* or *INCOMPLETE*.

The task for our classifier is to predict whether a given bug report is *Valid* or *Faulty*, based on a set of features that are comprised of different quantitative measures for the position of bug reporters in the collaboration network. In order to highlight the predictive power gained by the inclusion of further measures, we start with a very simple classifier which only considers the presence of a bug reporter in the network's largest connected component (LCC). We then incrementally add a prediction that is based on a threshold of eigenvector centrality as well as–eventually–a support vector machine that makes use of the following set of nine topological measures calculated at the level of a node: presence in the LCC, eigenvector, betweenness, and closeness centrality, local clustering coefficient, coreness, as well as in-, out- and total degree. Illustrative overviews of the three different classification schemes are provided in Figures 5.2(a) to 5.2(c). For each of the obtained classifiers, we evaluate its predictive power in terms of *precision, recall* and the corresponding *F*-score (equally weighted precision and recall) [110, 178]. In order to enable the reader to correctly interpret the predictive power based on the obtained precision and recall values, in the first line of Table 5.4 we indicate the actual fraction of *Valid* bug reports in our data set for each of the considered projects.

---

[1] *WONTFIX* is considered as valid because these are issues that can be fixed, even when irrelevant

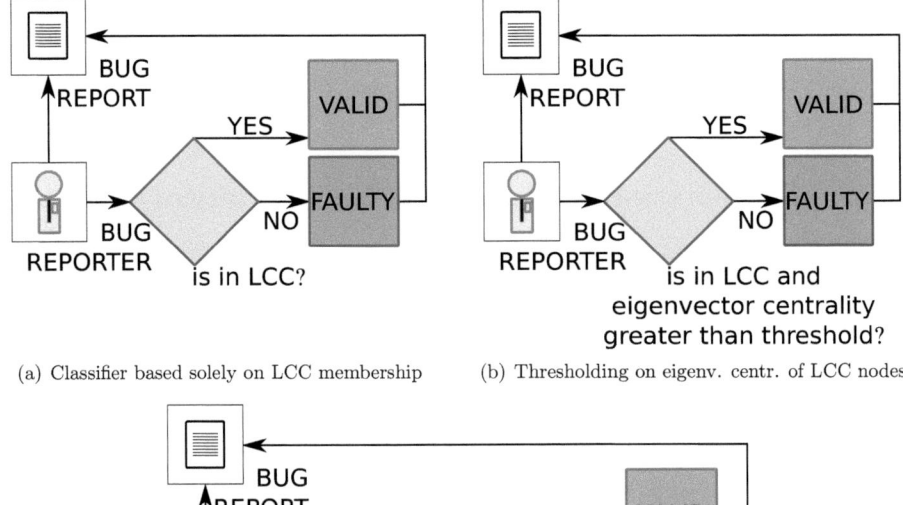
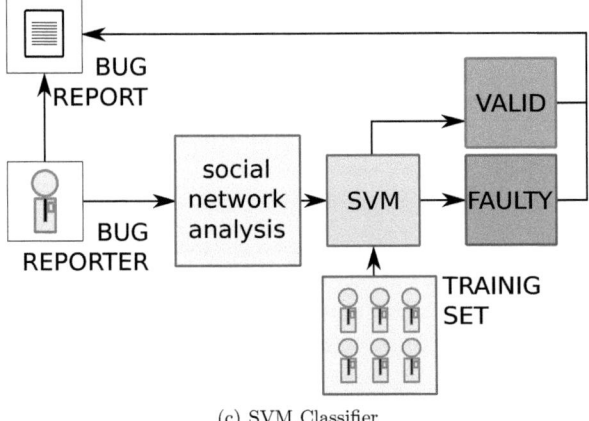

**Figure 5.2:** Graphical illustration of the three classifiers described in section 5.5. When bug reporters submit reports, we immediately quantify the nine measures that express their social embeddedness as described in the text. These are used as input to the classifier, which will then predict if bug reports are valid or faulty. For the case of the SVM classifier, we separate 5.0% of the samples to be used as training data.

We first consider a simple prediction method which considers a bug report to be valid whenever the bug reporter is in the LCC of the collaboration network in the month preceding the submission of the bug report. The basis for this prediction is provided in Table 5.3, which lists the fraction of bug reporters belonging to the LCC of the network individually for each of the different bug categories. In the two bottom rows, we furthermore

**Table 5.3:** Percentages of bug reporters that are in the LCC of the social network in the month preceding the report. The percentages given were calculated for each of the resolution categories (e.g. for FIREFOX, from those that reported bugs resolved as FIXED: 53.9% were in the LCC while 46.1% were not).

|        | FIREFOX | THUNDERBIRD | ECLIPSE | NETBEANS |
|--------|---------|-------------|---------|----------|
| FIX    | 53.9%   | 47.4%       | 64.0%   | 65.0%    |
| DUP    | 28.0%   | 9.4%        | 62.4%   | 42.7%    |
| INV    | 11.2%   | 8.6%        | 42.2%   | 46.7%    |
| WOF    | 37.7%   | 18.2%       | 52.9%   | 51.6%    |
| INC    | 4.1%    | 4.7%        | -       | 26.6%    |
| Valid  | 50.6%   | 44.1%       | 62.6%   | 62.2%    |
| Faulty | 17.2%   | 8.3%        | 56.1%   | 41.2%    |

provide the same values for the aggregated sets of *Valid* and *Faulty* bugs. For MOZILLA FIREFOX and MOZILLA THUNDERBIRD one observes a significant difference between these two categories, i.e. the fraction of reporters of *Valid* bugs that are in the LCC is significantly higher than the fraction of reporters of *Faulty* bugs. For ECLIPSE and NETBEANS the effect is less pronounced. Table 5.4 (see (LCC) labeled rows) shows the precision, recall and $F$-score of a classifier that is solely based on LCC membership. When comparing to the real proportion of *Valid* bug reports, this predictor clearly performs better than a null model of randomly sampling bug reports. Due to the stronger effect of LCC membership, the performance is clearly better for MOZILLA FIREFOX and MOZILLA THUNDERBIRD, which at the same time are the projects with the smallest proportion of *Valid* bug reports.

**Table 5.4:** Precision ($p$), recall ($r$) and $F$-score of filtering valid bug reports based only on measures of social embeddedness.

|             | FIREFOX | THUNDERBIRD | ECLIPSE | NETBEANS |
|-------------|---------|-------------|---------|----------|
| Valid       | 21.0%   | 23.3%       | 74.3%   | 62.4%    |
| $p$ (LCC)   | 44.1%   | 62.1%       | 76.3%   | 71.9%    |
| $r$ (LCC)   | 50.9%   | 44.5%       | 62.6%   | 62.4%    |
| $F$ (LCC)   | 0.47    | 0.52        | 0.69    | 0.67     |
| $p$ (evcent)| 60.4%   | 68.6%       | 76.3%   | 76.7%    |
| $r$ (evcent)| 30.5%   | 5.4%        | 62.6%   | 38.8%    |
| $F$ (evcent)| 0.41    | 0.10        | 0.69    | 0.52     |
| $p$ (SVM)   | 82.5%   | 90.3%       | 88.7%   | 78.9%    |
| $r$ (SVM)   | 44.5%   | 38.9%       | 91.0%   | 87.0%    |
| $F$ (SVM)   | 0.58    | 0.54        | 0.89    | 0.83     |

As the next measure we add to the classifier the eigenvector centrality of bug reporters. This classifier will mark bug reports as *Valid* if the reporter is part of the LCC and if their respective eigenvector centrality scores are above a precentile threshold that is tuned for each community individually. The results shown in Table 5.4 (see (evcent) labeled rows) indicate that–compared to a classification based on mere LCC membership–the inclusion of eigenvector centrality increases the precision while generally decreasing recall and $F$-

score. Due to the negative relation between eigenvector centrality and bug report quality found for MOZILLA THUNDERBIRD, the drop in the $F$-score is particularly pronounced for this project.

Our next and final step towards a practical tool is a) the use of a support vector machine (SVM) [102] for the prediction of *Valid* bug reports and b) the use of the full set of nine topological measures. In order to eliminate the risk of overfitting the data, we use a training set that is composed of only 5.0% of all available samples. The nine measures we consider as input features are: *LCC membership, eigenvector centrality, betweenness centrality, total degree, in-degree, out-degree, closeness centrality, clustering coefficient* and *k-coreness*. We present the results of the SVM classifier in Table 5.4 (see (SVM) labeled rows). For MOZILLA FIREFOX and MOZILLA THUNDERBIRD we obtain precision values of 82.5 and 90.3 as well as $F$-scores of 0.58 and 0.54 respectively. In both of these projects the fraction of *Valid* bug reports is comparably small (with 21% and 23.3% respectively).

The fraction of *Valid* bugs in the ECLIPSE and NETBEANS projects is significantly higher. We hypothesize that this is due to more stringent bug reporting procedures and a higher technical proficiency of contributors which is related to the fact that both projects target a community that mainly consists of developers. For ECLIPSE and NETBEANS our classifier obtains a precision of 88.7% and 78.9% with $F$-scores of 0.89 and 0.83 respectively. Since the majority of bug reports in these two projects are *Valid*, we propose to use the classifier to identify the minority of *Faulty* bug reports instead. In Table 5.5, we show the corresponding results for all four projects. In this setting, our classifier achieves $F$-scores of 0.92 and 0.91 and a precision of 86.9% and 84.9% for MOZILLA FIREFOX and MOZILLA THUNDERBIRD respectively. For the projects ECLIPSE and NETBEANS we obtain a precision of 73.6% and 73.1% and $F$-scores of 0.69 and 0.67 respectively.

**Table 5.5:** Precision ($p$), recall ($r$) and $F$-score of filtering faulty bug reports based only on measures of social embeddedness.

|         | FIREFOX | THUNDERBIRD | ECLIPSE | NETBEANS |
|---------|---------|-------------|---------|----------|
| Faulty  | 79.0%   | 76.7%       | 25.7%   | 37.6%    |
| $p$ (SVM) | 86.9% | 84.9%       | 73.6%   | 73.1%    |
| $r$ (SVM) | 97.3% | 98.2%       | 64.0%   | 61.8%    |
| $F$ (SVM) | 0.92  | 0.91        | 0.69    | 0.67     |

## 5.6 Threats to Validity

Prior to concluding this chapter, we discuss a number of limitations of our analysis as well as resulting threats to validity. As described in section 5.3, all our findings are based

## 5.6. THREATS TO VALIDITY 105

on interactions recorded in the BUGZILLA installation of the projects MOZILLA FIREFOX, MOZILLA THUNDERBIRD, ECLIPSE and NETBEANS. Clearly, a significant threat to the applicability of our approach for general collaborative software engineering is that we were mainly focused on these four OSS communities. However, we argue that these particular projects represent communities with different levels of heterogeneity with respect to the level of contributions, commitment, technical proficiency and commercial influence by companies. In particular, the communities of MOZILLA FIREFOX and MOZILLA THUNDERBIRD target a rather general audience without particular technical proficiency, while ECLIPSE and NETBEANS are more focused on software developers. As such, our particular choice of communities may be considered as covering different ends of the spectrum of technical proficiency of contributors. Our analysis shows that, even for such diverse projects, machine learning techniques based on quantitative measures of social embeddedness yield high accuracy results when predicting bug report quality. Therefore our contribution can be seen as a proof of concept case study. Nevertheless, we are currently collecting and analyzing data as well as qualitative insights on the social organization of a number of additional communities in order to generalize our results.

Although our analysis focuses on the BUGZILLA communities of OSS projects, our methodology is–in general–not limited to these. Any issue tracking system which records time-stamped direct interactions between its contributors can be used to extract evolving collaboration networks and thus to compute quantitative measures for social embeddedness. However, whether these measures can be used for highly accurate, automated bug categorization in settings other than the ones studied in this chapter (like e.g. commercial software production or collaborations in smaller or less diverse teams) requires further studies and is beyond the scope of our work.

While we have presented a set of quantitative results regarding the relation between the network position of bug reporters and the outcome of bug report processing, it is unclear what are the exact social mechanisms at work. In order to gain a better insight into this question, we have created a survey that was sent to the community managers of the projects considered in this case study. Indeed, in their replies the community managers of ECLIPSE and NETBEANS confirmed that such a relation may exist. Specifically, we received feedback indicating that for the NETBEANS community "one of the criteria developers use while choosing bugs for fixing is reproducible case and/or reputation of the reporter". Similarly, for the ECLIPSE project community managers confirmed that "a committer is often times more likely to spend triage time on a bug from somebody with a known reputation for quality". Unfortunately, we did not receive any feedback to our survey for the communities of MOZILLA FIREFOX and MOZILLA THUNDERBIRD.

For the network measures studied in this chapter, we only used the direct dyadic relations *CC* (i.e. contributors subscribing to receive information about future updates on bug reports) and *Assign* (i.e. contributors assigning the task of handling a bug to another one). While these recorded interactions are clearly associated with contributors knowing about and interacting with each other, the resulting network must clearly be seen as a mere proxy for the actual social organization of a community. In particular, in our study of network measures we did not consider further relations that may be extracted for instance from the sequence of comments on a bug. The reason for not considering these is the lower fidelity with respect to whether an extracted relation is really associated with direct communication or collaboration. Furthermore, in our study we so far did not use further potential data sources, like mailing lists or threaded forum communication that could be used to augment our network perspective in a subsequent analysis.

Another remark related to the measures of social embeddedness adopted in our analysis is that they can be quantified right away after a bug report is submitted. As we show in the chapter, this works well for OSS communities that have accumulated enough samples to apply machine learning techniques. Therefore the extension of this methodology to newly born communities remains a challenge.

A possible reason of concern is the fact that we use a fixed-size window of 30 days to construct the networks used in our analysis. Although we have obtained high accuracy results for this particular choice of window size, we are further investigating whether tuning this parameter to each community independently will further increase performance.

Finally, the application of machine learning comes at the risk of overfitting data by using a too large fraction of training data. In order to avoid this pitfall, we limited the fraction of randomly chosen training data to 5.0%. To foster the reproducibility of our results and to facilitate the implementation of similar approaches of social awareness in practical support infrastructures, the source code of the SVM classifier (written in the R language) as well as the data sets studied in our analysis are available online[2].

## 5.7 Conclusion

In this chapter we have studied to what extent the positions of bug reporters in the collaboration networks of four OSS communities are indicative for the quality of contributed bug reports. We have addressed this question from the perspective of evolving complex networks that have been extracted from a comprehensive data set on 700,000 bug reports

---

[2]see http://www.sg.ethz.ch/research/topics/social-se/data/

## 5.7. CONCLUSION

for the projects MOZILLA FIREFOX, MOZILLA THUNDERBIRD, ECLIPSE and NETBEANS. The main results of our case study on these communities are the following:

**(1)** We study the evolution of bug reporter centrality in *evolving collaboration networks*, using a time resolution of 30 days over a total period of 10 years. For the project MOZILLA FIREFOX, we are able to validate our hypothesis that the eigenvector centrality of bug reporters increases after the submission of valid bug reports (i.e. reports that refer to actual software bugs, are no duplicates and contain all necessary information). We observe the opposite relation for MOZILLA THUNDERBIRD.

**(2)** In all projects we were able to validate our hypothesis that there is a statistically significant decrease of eigenvector centrality following the submission of duplicate bugs.

**(3)** For the projects MOZILLA FIREFOX, MOZILLA THUNDERBIRD and NETBEANS we were able to validate our hypothesis that the eigenvector centrality of contributors reporting *Valid* bug reports is significantly higher than those of users submitting *Faulty* bug reports. From this we conclude that the position of bug reporters in the collaboration network of OSS communities is indicative for the quality of bug reports.

**(4)** Based on this finding, we develop an automated bug report classification mechanism. We use nine topological measures at the level of bug reporters (eigenvector, betweenness and closeness centrality, k-coreness, clustering coefficient, in-, out- and total degree as well as membership in the largest connected component) for the prediction of whether a reported bug is *Valid* or *Faulty*. Based on a support vector machine and depending on the project considered, our automated classification achieves a precision of up to 90.3% and an $F$-score of up to 0.92.

We would like to emphasize the fact that–although it is merely based on measures quantifying the network position of bug reporters–*our proposed classification mechanism achieves a remarkably high accuracy across different communities*. The combination of our approach with further features used in previous studies of automated bug classification is likely to further improve its accuracy. Our case study can thus be seen as a contribution towards classification schemes that are highly accurate, yet simple enough to be of practical relevance in the design of support infrastructures.

# Part II

# Software Modularity

"There's nothing in the universe cold steel won't cut"

Conan
*Beyond the Black River* (1935)

# Chapter 6

# Monitoring Software Modularity

### Summary

In this chapter, we borrow concepts from complex networks theory to quantify the congruence of the network of software dependencies and the modular decomposition of the source code. We perform an empirical study on a dataset consisting of 28 large open source JAVA projects and show that $Q$, a measure known from the study of modularity in complex networks, is a promising macroscopic approach to monitor source code evolution. Within this context, it can be used to increase the awareness of developers with respect to the deterioration of software modularity, by quantifying the impact of local development activity on the system as a whole.

## 6.1 Introduction

The modularity of a software architecture is considered a key feature that contributes to the sustainability of large scale software projects [160]. Ideally, modularization fosters the decoupling of software development efforts, which can then be performed independently if a binding standard interface is established. As the software evolves, modularity favors its maintainability and expandability [56, 133, 214]. If the development of a given system is meant to be sustainable, the amount of effort required to perform modifications in the software architecture must be compatible with the resources (e.g. time, human, etc) available at any time. Therefore monitoring the modularity of an evolving software system promises to be an important step towards a sustainable software development regime, however such a task would be tedious and slow if performed manually.

In this chapter, we propose quantitative approach to measure the congruence between the clusters in the network of software dependencies of large open source JAVA projects and their modular decomposition[1]. Our method is based on the well-established complex networks framework [4, 151]. In order to adopt this framework, the first necessary step is to restate software modules and software dependencies in terms of network structures [86, 111, 124, 149, 237].

Through a network perspective, it is straightforward to visualize that the expected functionality of a software module is provided by the cooperation between fundamental software constructs (e.g. functions, procedures, classes, files, etc). Therefore the challenge in software modularization consists in clustering dependent software constructs into software modules, by minimizing the number of dependencies between modules, while maximizing the number of dependencies within modules. This can be directly mapped to the software engineering literature, where software said to be modular is expected to have *cohesive* modules (dense network of intra-module dependencies), while remaining sparsely *coupled* (sparse network of inter-module dependencies) [87]. The relevance of this premise is clear: when followed as a design principle, it yields architectures that are easier to maintain, for example, by allowing the simple replacement of obsolete modules.

Our contribution is based on a quantitative approach expressing the congruence between the decomposition of a software system into software modules and the cluster structures found in the network of software dependencies. Here, we do not attempt to construct module decompositions that optimize the congruence with respect to the software dependencies (this is addressed in Chapter 7). We only monitor the software modularity of a

---

[1] JAVA was not designed with an abstraction for *modules*, but we argue in section 6.2 that JAVA *packages* are a reasonable approximation

system already decomposed into modules. We argue that our method can measure how software modularity is affected by modifications made to the source code at the level of the software dependencies. To illustrate the dynamics of this process, we study the dynamics of software modularity as expressed with this quantitative approach, in a case study considering the revision control logs of 28 open source JAVA projects. We argue that our approach provides valuable insights into the related software engineering processes and the sustainability of large scale projects.

In section 6.2 we present our methodology. Section 6.3 discusses our results and in section 6.4 we comment on related work, while in section 6.5 we discuss the validity of our approach. Finally, in section 6.6 we conclude our work and we then elaborate on further research ideas.

## 6.2 Methodology

The starting point of our methodology is the reexpression of software dependencies in terms of a network structure. Conceptually, such an approach will vary accordingly to the targeted programming language or programming paradigm. We choose to focus our efforts on software written in JAVA, for the latter is a very popular programming language among free and open source software developers. Therefore, plenty of examples containing the complete source code evolution are available in online software repositories[2]. JAVA source code can be easily reinterpreted in terms of network structures: JAVA classes are taken as network *nodes*, while a network *link* will connect any two nodes if the corresponding JAVA classes share at least one software dependency (e.g. reference to method or attribute, inheritance, function call, etc). Finally, JAVA was not designed with a specific abstraction for modules[3] [99]. However, JAVA allows *classes* to be group into namespaces that are called *packages*. It is considered good practice to organize these packages following modularity principles: high intra-package cohesion and low inter-package coupling[4] [5, 19, 103]. We adopt the same approach and consider JAVA package as a reasonable approximation for modules.

Figure 6.1 presents a visual example of a software dependency network resulting from the application of this method to one of the versions of the source code of ASPECTJ (a JAVA framework supporting the implementation of software using the aspect-oriented programming paradigm [72]). In our dataset, this network grows from 654 up to 1,651 nodes

---
[2]e.g. SOURCEFORGE http://sourceforge.net/
[3]http://branchandbound.net/blog/java/2013/07/java-modularity-story/
[4]http://www.javapractices.com/topic/TopicAction.do?Id=205

**Figure 6.1:** Visualization of the software dependency network of AspectJ as of 01-Aug-2004, showing only the largest connected component. This visualization was generated with Gephi [17].

(Java classes). Each color represents a single module (Java package). Thus, two classes bearing the same color are members of the same package. Similar software dependency networks can be extracted from software written with different programming languages and paradigms. See the examples in [111, 149].

As demonstrated in Figure 6.1, the visualization of software dependency networks is a very useful technique in the analysis of the software modularity. However, a quantitative

## 6.2. METHODOLOGY

approach is still desirable since it allows us to capture the structural organization of a network in terms of a single number. This can be used to analyze the evolution of a modular software architecture and can also be applied in a statistical correlation analysis when considering different quantitative measures.

In recent years, the network sciences community has developed a number of quantitative measures which capture structural features like e.g. clusters, as well as the impact of any other structural entities on dynamical processes like e.g. information or failure spreading, consensus, opinion formation or synchronization [152]. According to our needs, we adopt a network measure which was first used to study assortative mixing in networks. This represents the tendency for network nodes to be connected to other nodes that are similar (i.e. assortative) or dissimilar (i.e. disassorative) to them in some way [150]. Assuming that sharing the same module membership makes nodes similar (and dissimilar otherwise), this measure could then be used to quantify the modularity of network structures [153]. For a given network of software dependencies, such that each network node is assigned to a given module[5], its degree of software modularity is defined by

$$Q = \frac{\sum_i^n e_{ii} - \sum_i^n a_i b_i}{1 - \sum_i^n a_i b_i} \qquad (6.1)$$

where $e_{ij}$ is the fraction of links that connect nodes in module $i$ to nodes in module $j$, $a_i = \sum_j^n e_{ij}$ and $b_i = \sum_j^n e_{ji}$ are the column and row sum respectively, while $n$ corresponds to the number of modules. If the network is undirected, the matrix defined by **e** is symmetric and $a_i = b_i$ [150]. We use $Q$ to measure the fraction of links that connect nodes within the same module ($\sum_i^n e_{ii}$) minus the value of the same quantity expected from a randomized network ($\sum_i^n a_i b_i$). If the former is not better than random $Q = 0$ [153]. However, $Q$ would not be defined if all links are concentrated within a single module. For such trivial case, the scaling factor equals zero ($1 - \sum_i^n a_i b_i = 1 - 1 = 0$). To avoid such a division by zero, we define $Q = 0$. In general, $Q \in [-1, 1]$. That is, the less coupled the modules and the higher their cohesion, the closer $Q$ is to 1. Figure 6.2 provides two examples of networks and their respective $Q$ scores. In the analysis of software structures, this measure is useful because in many cases the definition of modules is given by means of programming constructs like classes, files, namespaces or packages, etc. With this, $Q$ can be used to study how well the cluster structures in the network of dependencies correspond to the modular decomposition of a project. We apply it in an analysis of the dynamics of software modularity of JAVA open source projects and we discuss our results in section 6.3.

---

[5]modules and modular decomposition are defined "a priori"

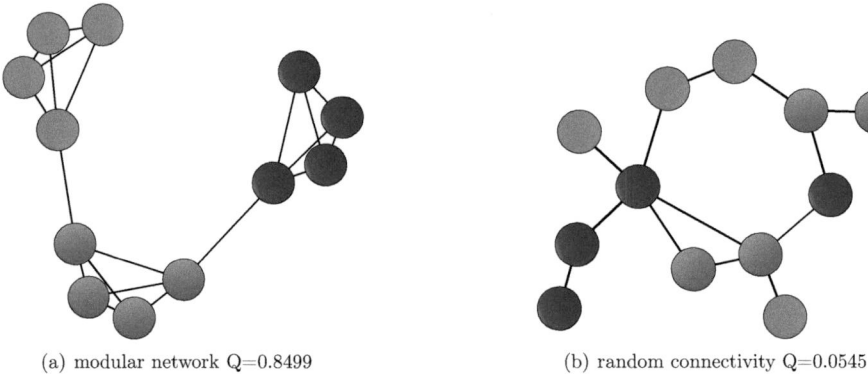

(a) modular network Q=0.8499      (b) random connectivity Q=0.0545

**Figure 6.2:** Two examples of undirected networks where nodes (i.e. circles) with the same color are members of the same module.

## 6.3 Results

Our analysis is based on a dataset containing the detailed source code evolution of 28 open source JAVA projects. The snapshots of the source code of each project were extracted from the respective CVS logs, on a monthly basis. Table 6.1 displays the recorded period of each project. Most of those projects are hosted at SOURCEFORGE and were selected because they were the largest (number of classes) at the time the dataset was collected. The single exception is ECLIPSE, which has its own repository [86]. The source code of ECLIPSE was thus obtained through a different setup. For each project, the CVS logs are processed, yielding software dependency networks stored in a directed graph format ($c_1$, $c_2$, $p_1$, $p_2$, $t$) which reads as: class $c_1$ from package $p_1$ depends on class $c_2$ from package $p_2$ at time $t$. Furthermore, we only focus on syntactic dependencies which are obtained using the abstract syntax tree parser JDT [86]. Using the schema described in section 6.2, we apply $Q$ to the network extracted from each snapshot within the recorded period. In order to facilitate the presentation of the evolution of these projects, we aggregate, and sort by time stamp $t$, all snapshots of each project. We compute the mean fluctuation in time ($< Q(t+1) - Q(t) >, \forall t$) for all consecutive snapshots of the software. This approach captures the average incremental change of the $Q$ over the observation period. We also compute the respective standard deviation ($\sigma(Q(t+1) - Q(t)), \forall t$), which captures the degree of fluctuation of the changes in modularity over the same period. We rank the projects according to the *mean* and *standard deviation* defined above, and we depict the result in Figure 6.3.

## 6.3. RESULTS

**Table 6.1:** The 28 JAVA projects which compose our source code evolution dataset.

| project name | record start | record end | project name | record start | record end |
|---|---|---|---|---|---|
| architecturware | 2004-04-01 | 2007-12-01 | jnode | 2003-06-01 | 2005-12-01 |
| aspectj | 2003-01-01 | 2008-02-01 | jpox | 2003-09-01 | 2006-12-01 |
| azureus | 2003-08-01 | 2008-01-01 | openqrm | 2007-04-01 | 2008-03-01 |
| cjos | 2000-11-01 | 2007-12-01 | openuss | 2003-06-01 | 2006-12-01 |
| composestar | 2003-12-01 | 2005-12-01 | openxava | 2004-12-01 | 2007-12-01 |
| eclipse | 2001-05-01 | 2008-03-01 | personalaccess | 2004-11-01 | 2007-12-01 |
| enterprise | 2002-11-01 | 2007-12-01 | phpeclipse | 2002-08-01 | 2007-12-01 |
| findbugs | 2003-04-01 | 2007-12-01 | rodin-b-sharp | 2005-11-01 | 2007-12-01 |
| fudaa | 2003-02-01 | 2007-12-01 | sapia | 2002-12-01 | 2007-12-01 |
| gpe4gtk | 2005-08-01 | 2006-12-01 | sblim | 2001-07-01 | 2007-12-01 |
| hibernate | 2001-12-01 | 2005-12-01 | springframework | 2003-03-01 | 2007-12-01 |
| jaffa | 2003-03-01 | 2007-12-01 | squirrel-sql | 2001-12-01 | 2007-12-01 |
| jena | 2001-02-01 | 2008-02-01 | xmsf | 2004-02-01 | 2007-12-01 |
| jmlspecs | 2002-03-01 | 2007-12-01 | yale | 2002-04-01 | 2008-02-01 |

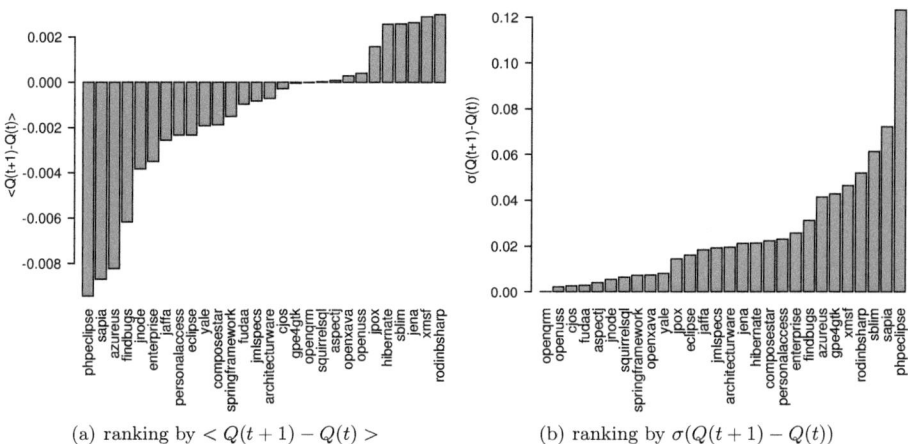

(a) ranking by $< Q(t+1) - Q(t) >$  (b) ranking by $\sigma(Q(t+1) - Q(t))$

**Figure 6.3:** Ranking software projects using the dynamics of $Q$.

According to the ranking in Figure 6.3(a), we divide our dataset into four groups of projects. This facilitates the visualization of their dynamics in terms of software modularity, as shown in Figure 6.4. Here, we observe that $Q$ effectively classifies projects according to different dynamic regimes. In Figure 6.3(a) we can focus in those projects that increase or decrease the software modularity the most, while in Figure 6.3(b) we can focus in the most dynamical or the most stable software development regimes.

In the following, we discuss in more detail two projects with contrasting dynamics in terms of $Q$. In particular, we focus on the the project AZUREUS, which is a torrent client (significant average decrease in $Q$), as well as JENA, a framework for building semantic web applications [144] (significant average increase in $Q$). In Figure 6.5, the time trajectory of the dynamics of $Q$ is shown for both projects as a function of project size (i.e. number of classes). We select three snapshots of the network of software dependencies of each of these two projects to illustrate their growth and its impact on modularity.

The respective software dependency networks are shown in Figure 6.6 and Figure 6.7. These networks have been created according to the methodology described in section 6.2, where each node represents a JAVA class, while a link represents a syntactic dependency (e.g. function call, inheritance, attribute reference, etc). Furthermore, in the network diagram nodes are colored according to package membership: same color, same package membership. In order to visualize the coherence between the package decomposition of the classes and the modular organization of the dependency network, each network diagram is generated with the force-directed Yifan-Hu layout algorithm [114]. This distributes nodes' spatial coordinates according to cluster structures. In particular, nodes in networks with highly modular structures will be densely clustered in the resulting layouts and the modules will become clearly distinguishable. In the resulting networks, we obtain a visual impression of the congruence between packages and clusters of dependencies as expressed quantitatively by $Q$ (see Figure 6.5).

The effect of the different dynamical regimes in terms of the evolution of $Q$ can easily be seen in the respective network structures. For the AZUREUS project, which is shown is Figures 6.6(a)–6.6(c), the coherence of the modular structure of the network of software dependencies with the package decomposition actually worsens over time, thus making it difficult to clearly separate packages in the resulting networks. On the contrary, the evolution of the JENA project shows a very different dynamics. While the growth in terms of the number of nodes and dependencies is in the same order of magnitude, the project maintains and even improves its modular decomposition, as is clearly shown in the figures 6.7(a)–6.7(c). From a software engineering perspective, the structure of JENA shown in Figure 6.7(c) is favorable, since it allows for an easy decomposition, maintenance and replacement of individual packages. One of the possible reasons for the discrepancy between JENA and AZUREUS is that the first is a framework aimed at an audience of developers. Thus, its structure must be well organized to facilitate its adoption, while the second is an end-user application and therefore the focus is on functionality rather than structural quality and clarity. Prior to concluding this chapter and discussing future

## 6.3. RESULTS

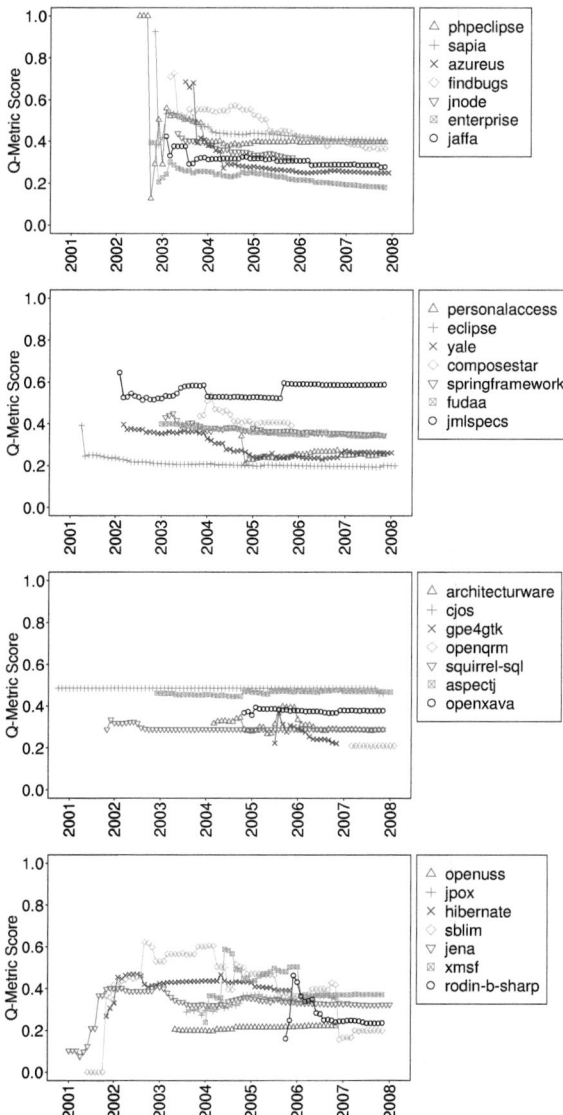

**Figure 6.4:** Dynamics of $Q$ in each project of our dataset. The projects are sorted according to $<Q(t+1) - Q(t)>$, and displayed in increasing order of magnitude (top-to-bottom). (top) highest mean decrease in $Q$. (bottom) highest mean increase in $Q$.

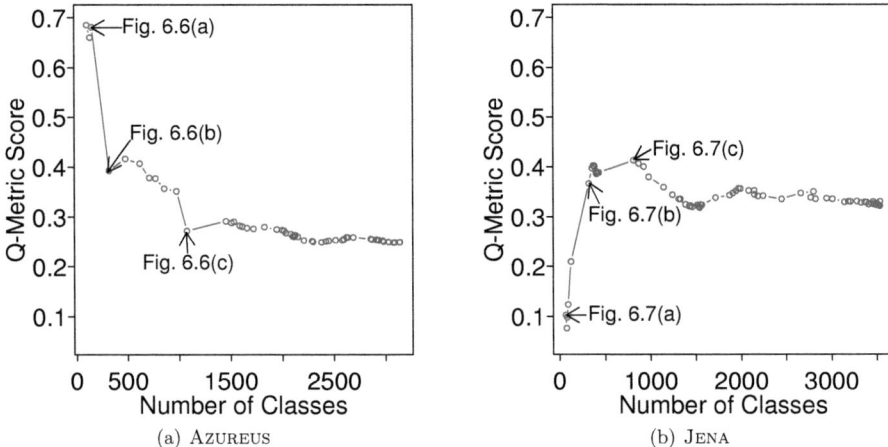

**Figure 6.5:** Detailed dynamics of $Q$ for the projects AZUREUS and JENA.

research, in the next section we comment on related work.

## 6.4 Related Work

One of the eye catching features of the dynamics of $Q$, as presented in Figure 6.4, is the large fluctuation of $Q$ at early stages of the project development. This is in accordance with results reported in [208]. There, it was shown that young open source projects display an accelerated growth rate while mature projects stabilize their dynamics and can grow further in a sustainable regime.

Another possible, complementary, reason for fluctuations are refactoring events, where software is usually rewritten or restructured in order to improve multiple features such as functionality, flexibility, reusability or structural quality. Such events could lead to the sudden jumps observed in Figure 6.4 along the time dynamics of a software project. In [57], refactoring metrics are proposed which take into account the dynamics of changing code. This line of research is well aligned with our purposes and can be easily adapted and augmented by our network perspective on software development processes.

For an early attempt of the application of network science to the analysis of software engineering processes we recommend [149], which also contains a short review of classical approaches used in the software engineering literature. Finally, in [73] a similar network

6.4. RELATED WORK 121

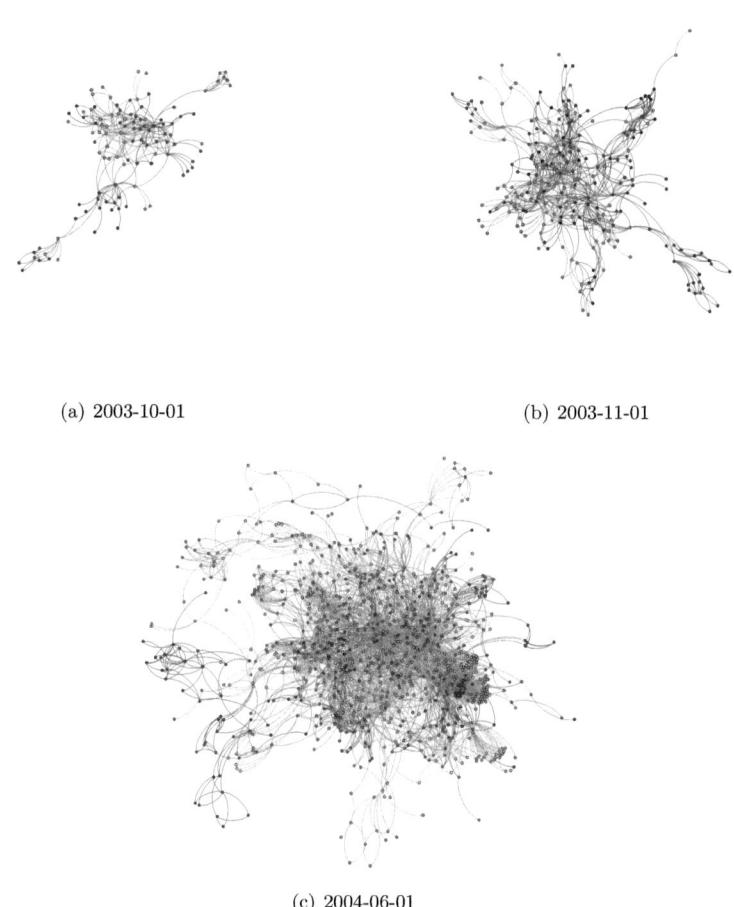

(a) 2003-10-01  (b) 2003-11-01

(c) 2004-06-01

**Figure 6.6:** Three snapshots of the dependency networks of the project AZUREUS. Same colors in the individual networks indicate same module (i.e. JAVA package) membership.

approach, though with a different measure, was used to study modularity of code and its relation to module survival. The authors draw a parallel to ecological systems and make use of a predator-prey model variation.

122                CHAPTER 6.  MONITORING SOFTWARE MODULARITY

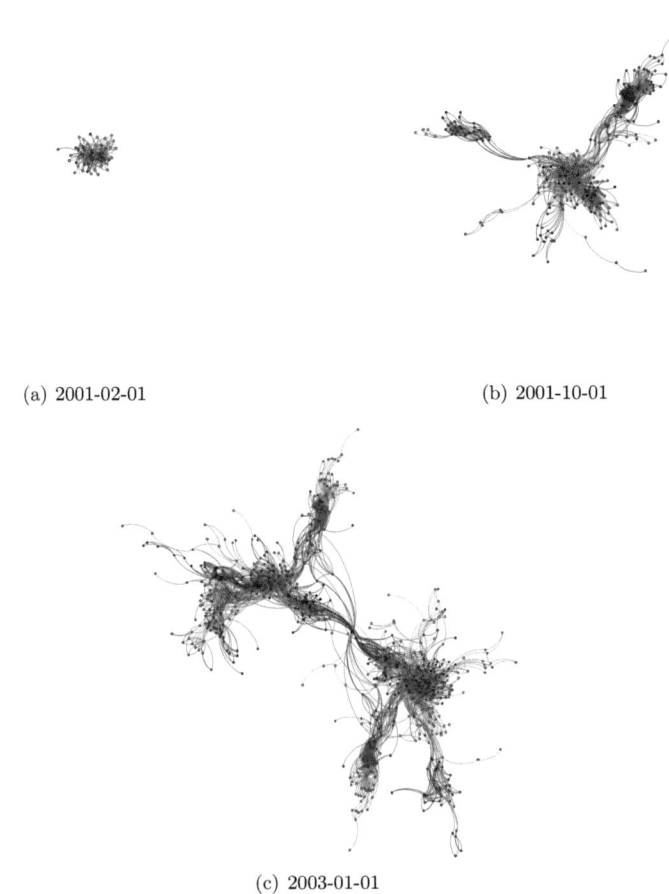

(a) 2001-02-01     (b) 2001-10-01

(c) 2003-01-01

**Figure 6.7:**  Three snapshots of the dependency networks of the project JENA.

## 6.5  Threats to Validity

As discussed above, JAVA does not support modularity in its design [99]. Using packages as modules is just a simple proxy to enable the application of our methodology [19]. Therefore, the results presented in this chapter only holds for this scenario. However, we argue that the use of $Q$ is valid and can generalize to other notions of modular decomposition.

Although $Q$ offers interesting insights, a known issue is that it is being influenced by intra-module dependencies. However it would be more thoughtful to place more weight on the impact of inter-module dependencies because these are the most relevant dependencies in a software modular structure.

Finally, we construct software dependency networks which only consider syntactic dependencies. The literature argues that for very large systems, *logical* dependencies should also be considered [77].

## 6.6 Conclusion

The results presented in this chapter indicate that $Q$, known from the analysis of cluster structures in network science, is a promising and reasonable approach to quantify the coherence between the module decomposition of large software projects and their dependency structures. As such, it constitutes a macroscopic measure that allows us to monitor and evaluate software engineering processes and reason about the sustainability of software architectures as they grow. In particular, it provides a simple mapping from local development activities (microscopic dynamics) to their respective impact on large scale structures of software systems.

Our study foreshadows a number of interesting research questions: How does the dynamics of $Q$ impact the sustainability of distributed software engineering efforts? Can the incorporation of such macroscopic measures into software development tools improve the design and maintenance of software architectures? How is the dynamics of $Q$ over the lifetime of software projects correlated with software development acts like refactoring or bug fixing? How is it correlated with social aspects, coordination acts or communication processes taking place between developers? Intuitively, one would assume that a reasonable modular decomposition of complex software systems facilitates distributed development processes and mitigates change propagation between interdependent modules. An interesting future work is to complement the methodology presented in this chapter with data on coordination and communication acts in the respective projects. In this line of arguments, a further interesting question is whether the pronouncedness of modular structures in the dependency network allows us to infer statements about the hierarchical organization of development teams.

While the exploration of these questions in this study has been necessarily incomplete, we argue that the associated line of research is a good demonstration for the potential impact of complex systems science on the engineering of complex software systems.

In Chapter 7, we extend the methodology presented here and propose an automated strategy to improve software modularity based on *move refactoring*. In our approach, the latter consists in redistributing JAVA classes across packages such that intra-package cohesion is maximized while minimizing inter-package coupling.

# Chapter 7

# Improving Software Modularity

Summary

In Chapter 6 we show that source code can evolve in ways that deteriorate software modularity. While many software systems are initially created in a modular way, over time modularity typically degrades as components are reused outside the context where they were created. Development costs might increase as the source code loses in comprehensibility, maintainability and thus quality. In this chapter, we propose an automated strategy to remodularize software based on *move refactoring*, e.g. moving JAVA classes between packages without changing any other aspect of the source code. Taking a complex systems perspective, our approach is based on complex networks theory applied to the dynamics of modular software structures and the relation to an $n$-state spin model known as the *Potts Model*. In our approach, nodes are probabilistically moved between modules with a probability that nonlinearly depends on number and module membership of their adjacent neighbors, which are defined by the underlying network of software dependencies. To validate our method, we apply it to a dataset of 39 JAVA open source projects in order to optimize their modularity. Comparing the source code generated by the developers with the optimized code resulting from our approach, we find that modularity (quantified in terms of $Q$, as discussed in Chapter 6) improves on average by $166 \pm 77$ percent. In order to facilitate the adoption of our method, we provide a freely available ECLIPSE plug-in.

## 7.1 Introduction

The modular design of complex software systems is an important factor that contributes to the success of software engineering projects. It is enabled by a set of design principles, among which *information hiding* and *separation of concerns* are the most influential ones [61, 159, 160, 199]. These two principles translate into commissioning different modules to different purposes, such that their internal implementation is transparent to developers making use of their functionalities. This approach has been shown to limit necessary coordination efforts and fosters the simple replacement of obsolete software modules by new ones [29, 217], thus bearing great relevance to the maintenance of sustainable software engineering regimes [209, 237].

In the modular design of software the question about the right level of granularity for a module is quite important. Ideally, to represent a reasonable *module*, a software component should be composed of a *highly cohesive* set of interdependent subcomponents which cannot be easily separated into smaller modules. At the same time, to represent a separate module, such a software component should exhibit a reasonably *low degree of coupling* to other modules. The goal of designing a modular software architecture in which modules exhibit at the same time *high cohesion* and *low coupling* is often achieved in the design phase of a project. However, empirical studies have shown that modularity often deteriorates throughout the subsequent phase of extending and maintaining a software [237, 242]. Hence, in order to retain the favorable properties of a modular design, remodularization strategies are needed. They rely on software restructuring known as *refactoring* [74].

In this chapter, we address the question how automated suggestions for refactoring can be used to improve the modularity of code. In order to minimize the impact on the actual code structures, and thus simplify the application of our approach in practical settings, we focus on the particular type of *move refactoring*, in which software constructs are moved between modules without changing other aspects of the source code. If these move refactorings are applied in such a way that the cohesion within modules increases, while the coupling between modules decreases, the modularity of the software improves without affecting the behavior and functionality of the software. While move refactoring is considered as a standard technique to remodularize software, approaches in the literature emphasize difficulties in its practical application that are due to cascades of subsequent move refactorings triggered by the moving of a single software construct [34, 64]. To avoid this caveat, we take a complex systems perspective and frame the remodularization of software based on move refactoring with a scheme similar to simulated annealing [122], in which the system is driven to an equilibrium state [20] by simple local changes. Based on this view, we derive a stochastic optimization algorithm which automates remodularization via move refactoring and validate it in a empirical study on the source code of 39 JAVA open source projects. We show that this approach creates software structures that have higher modularity than the original architectures extracted from the aforementioned empirical dataset. We further show that the achievable gain in modularity is related to the level of modularity in the initial architecture, hence indicating the presence of a significant modularization potential in architectures that exhibit low modularity. Although focused in software written in JAVA, we argue that our methodology can be easily extended to other programming languages and paradigms. To foster the reproduction of our results and catalyze their potential impact, we also provide a software prototype of our implementation as an ECLIPSE plug-in.

The rest of this chapter is organized as follows: we present our methodology in section 7.2, discuss our results in section 7.3, relate our approach to previous works in section 7.5, and present our conclusion in section 7.6.

## 7.2 Methods

In this section we describe the steps required to understand and reproduce our results. We start with our empirical datasets, then we move to the interpretation of software constructs and their dependencies in terms of the network structures manipulated during our remodularization strategy, followed by the description of its algorithm. We take inspiration from complex networks theory and apply the Newman's $Q$ modularity measure introduced in Chapter 6 to score the congruence between coupling and cohesion in a given modular decomposition and finally, we introduce the prototype of an ECLIPSE plug-in implementing a framework that will be expanded to include other approaches, fostering future research on this topic.

### 7.2.1 Datasets

We consider two distinct datasets. The first is composed of a curated collection of official releases of 14 JAVA open source software (*OSS*) projects, with a minimum of at least 10 releases each. These releases include the source code as well as the compiled binaries. This dataset is known as QUALITAS CORPUS [206]. The second dataset is composed of 28 JAVA OSS projects, for which fine grained CVS repository logs are available. The logs are aggregated over periods of 30 days such that each aggregation constitutes a full release of the given project. This dataset was previously used in [85, 86, 242] and in Chapter 6, and it was not updated due to the fact that for most of these projects, the development on CVS repositories became obsolete. In Table 7.1, we present the list of projects, the respective number of snapshots and the date corresponding to the last one.

### 7.2.2 Software Dependency Networks

In the following description, we focus on software written in JAVA. However, our approach can be applied right away to software projects developed in other programming languages and paradigms that have suitable abstractions for *modules* and *dependencies*. In particular, we assume that dependencies between packages represent the *coupling* between modules (see discussion in section 6.2). In particular, in the case of JAVA, we assume that a package $A$ depends on a package $B$ when a JAVA class (i.e. network node) $a$ in $A$ depends on a class $b$ in $B$. Here, dependency stands for any kind of relationship between classes such as inheritance, as well as a reference to attributes or methods. A single link between $a$ and $b$ is created if there is at least one such dependency[1]. By this definition a package is highly cohesive when its classes are tightly connected. Similar approaches were applied in [19, 242]. Figure 7.1 provides an illustration of our method.

In order to extract such dependency networks (also known as call graphs) from the OSS projects found in the QUALITAS CORPUS dataset, we use a customized version of an OSS parser called DEPENDENCYFINDER [207]. An alternative approach is used to parse the dataset composed of CVS logs. For regular intervals of 30 days, we check out all the corresponding logs and aggregate them, resulting in monthly releases. The dependency network is then extracted by employing the abstract syntax tree parser JDT. For both datasets, the output of this process is a list of links of the form $a, b, A, B$, meaning class $a$, which belongs to package $A$, depends on a class $b$ found in package $B$.

### 7.2.3 A Complex Systems Approach to ReModularization

Our approach to remodularization is based on *move refactoring*, a technique to reorganize source code which does not modify neither the software dependency network, nor the behavior or functionality of the software itself. As an example, consider the modular software system (e.g. written in an object oriented programming language) which is illustrated in Figure 7.2(a). This system is composed of three coupled modules $A$, $B$ and $C$. As described in section 7.2.2, these dependencies are the result of the interaction between the classes within each module, which can be located internally (intra-module dependencies)

---

[1] in this *simplification* links have no weights, but we argue that it can be generalized to weighted links

**Table 7.1:** Our datasets of JAVA OSS projects. For the QUALITAS CORPUS dataset, the column "Snapshots" indicate the number of releases of a given project, while in the case of CVS logs it indicates the number of monthly snapshots aggregated over the recorded project history.

| | QUALITAS CORPUS | |
|---|---|---|
| Project | Snapshots | Last Snapshot Date |
| ANT | 21 | 2010-12-27 |
| ANTLR | 20 | 2011-07-18 |
| ARGOUML | 16 | 2011-12-15 |
| AZUREUS | 57 | 2011-12-02 |
| ECLIPSE_SDK | 40 | 2011-09-10 |
| FREECOL | 28 | 2011-09-27 |
| FREEMIND | 16 | 2011-02-19 |
| HIBERNATE | 100 | 2012-02-08 |
| JGRAPH | 39 | 2009-09-28 |
| JMETER | 20 | 2011-09-29 |
| JUNG | 23 | 2010-01-25 |
| JUNIT | 23 | 2011-09-29 |
| LUCENE | 28 | 2011-11-20 |
| WEKA | 55 | 2011-10-28 |

| | CVS logs | |
|---|---|---|
| Project | Snapshots | Last Snapshot Date |
| ARCHITECTURWARE | 46 | 2008-02-04 |
| ASPECTJ | 62 | 2008-02-01 |
| AZUREUS | 54 | 2008-01-01 |
| CJOS | 87 | 2008-02-04 |
| COMPOSESTAR | 26 | 2008-07-04 |
| ECLIPSE | 83 | 2008-03-01 |
| ENTERPRISE | 64 | 2008-02-04 |
| FINDBUGS | 58 | 2008-02-04 |
| FUDAA | 60 | 2008-07-01 |
| GPE4GTK | 18 | 2008-07-04 |
| HIBERNATE | 50 | 2008-02-04 |
| JAFFA | 59 | 2008-01-28 |
| JENA | 86 | 2008-02-01 |
| JMLSPECS | 71 | 2008-01-28 |
| JNODE | 32 | 2008-02-03 |
| JPOX | 41 | 2008-01-28 |
| OPENQRM | 13 | 2008-03-01 |
| OPENUSS | 44 | 2008-07-01 |
| OPENXAVA | 38 | 2008-02-04 |
| PERSONALACCESS | 39 | 2008-07-04 |
| PHPECLIPSE | 66 | 2008-07-04 |
| RODINBSHARP | 27 | 2008-07-04 |
| SAPIA | 62 | 2008-07-01 |
| SBLIM | 79 | 2008-07-01 |
| SPRINGFRAMEWORK | 59 | 2008-02-03 |
| SQUIRRELSQL | 74 | 2008-07-04 |
| XMSF | 48 | 2008-07-04 |
| YALE | 71 | 2008-02-01 |

```
package A;
import B.*;
import C.*;

public class a extends b{
    public static void main (String[] args) {
        c object_c = new c();
        object_c.runMethod();
        ...
    }
    ...
}
package C;
import D.*;

public class c{
    public static void main (String[] args) {
        d object_d = new d();
        object_d.runMethod();
        ...
    }
    ...
}
```

(a) JAVA source code excerpt

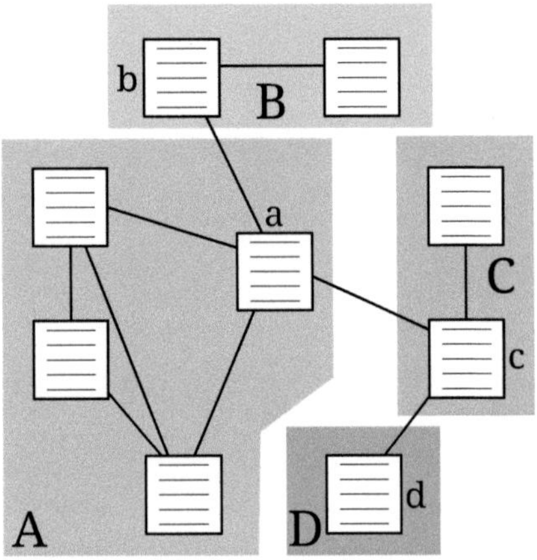

(b) corresponding dependency network

**Figure 7.1:** Example of a modular software. (a) Source code excerpt. (b) Corresponding undirected network structure. The shaded areas represent modules (e.g. JAVA packages), which are internally composed of software constructs (e.g. JAVA classes). Links between such elements indicate structural dependencies (e.g. class inheritance, reference to attribute or method, etc).

or across different modules (inter-module coupling). Too much inter-module coupling hinders modular architectures. For example, in terms of developer cognition, highly coupled modules cannot be easily isolated, forcing the developer to go over all the inter-module dependencies in order to understand the functionalities of a single module. In summary, the more coupling exists between modules, the harder it becomes to maintain and expand the software.

*Move refactoring* offers a simple solution to this problem. It consists of moving software constructs within a module to adjacent modules without changing the dependency structure of the software. In terms of the example discussed above, by carefully moving classes from their original modules into other modules, it is possible to reduce the coupling between modules. Thus, move refactoring applied to a software dependency network translates into relabeling the network nodes (e.g JAVA classes) according to module membership (e.g. JAVA package membership). In Figure 7.2, we illustrate the result of five move refactorings involving a single class each (the classes are $a1, a2, b1, c1, c2$). The modules in the refactored system, represented by Figure 7.2(b), are indeed less coupled. It is important to note that when moving content around, while ignoring the semantics of each module, it is likely that the principle of separation of concerns will be violated [61, 159, 199]. We address this issue in section 7.3.

For small systems, such as the one illustrated in Figure 7.2, move refactoring is a trivial task and can be performed manually. Due to the structural complexity of software, the larger the system, the harder it is for a developer to grasp which could be suitable move refactoring steps. As described in section 7.5, most of the literature addresses this issue by means of optimization techniques. In most of these techniques, every possible move needs to be scored by the evaluation of a global optimization criterion (e.g. an *objective function* quantifying coupling and cohesion). In this chapter, we propose a stochastic move refactoring strategy that does not require to keep track of such optimization criteria[2]. Besides providing an interesting, new, and simpler, perspective on remodularization based on complex system theory, our approach also addresses concerns in the literature regarding the explicit use of coupling-cohesion metrics when guiding the optimization search.

Our algorithm works as follows: For a modular system composed of $n$ packages and $k$ classes, at each time step, we pick a class $c$ at random and count the number of links $N_j^{(c)}$ connecting it to other classes in each package $j$, such that $j \in \{module(c')|c' \in \mathcal{N}(c)\}$. Here, $\mathcal{N}(c)$ represents the set of classes adjacent to $c$ (or in other words, the neighborhood

---

[2]see Algorithm 1

of $c$). The probability $P_j^{(c)}$ that this class will be moved to package $j$ is

$$P_j^{(c)} = \frac{\exp\left(N_j^{(c)}/T\right)}{\sum_{i=1}^{n}\exp\left(N_i^{(c)}/T\right)}. \tag{7.1}$$

Thus, this randomly picked class has higher probability to be moved into a package where it maintains most of its connections. Indeed, this could be its current package. In such a case this class has higher probability to not undergo move refactoring. The *temperature* parameter $T$ (constant) controls the likelihood of moves that would deteriorate the modularity of this architecture. This deterioration is characterized by the increase of the number of inter-module links if "bad" moves actually occur. The smaller $T$, the smaller the chance to select such move refactorings. Although small, this probability is not zero. This nonvanishing probability fosters the exploration of rugged problem landscapes, allowing the search to escape local optima.

From a computational point of view, it is worth remarking that (for projects with large number of classes) the exponential term $\exp\left(N_j^{(c)}/T\right)$ may yield an out-of-bounds error because of numerical precision. In order to avoid this, we can find $N_{max}^{(c)} = \arg\max_{l \in [1,n]} N_l^{(c)}$, i.e. the maximum number of nodes connected to $c$ by inter-module links. Then, we compute

$$P_j^{(c)} = \frac{\exp\left(-\frac{N_{max}^{(c)}-N_j^{(c)}}{T}\right)}{\sum_{i=1}^{n}\exp\left(-\frac{N_{max}^{(c)}-N_i^{(c)}}{T}\right)}, \tag{7.2}$$

which is equivalent to Eq. 7.1, and each exponential term is smaller than one.

To summarize, at each step we perform a move refactoring iteration according to the probability distribution $P$. This procedure is repeated for a finite number of steps. Algorithm 1 presents the pseudocode of our stochastic move refactoring strategy, while in Figure 7.3 we illustrate one step of this algorithm.

In statistical physics, the model described by Eq. 7.1 is similar to the $n$-state *Potts Model* [231]. In a fully connected graph, this system is a paradigmatic model to study the equilibrium phase transition (as a function of temperature) from an ordered state, where all the nodes reside in the same module–to a disordered one–where all the nodes are randomly located in different modules. In the case of complex topologies–like those found in class dependencies–the equilibrium configuration will depend on the modular coherence

## 7.2. METHODS

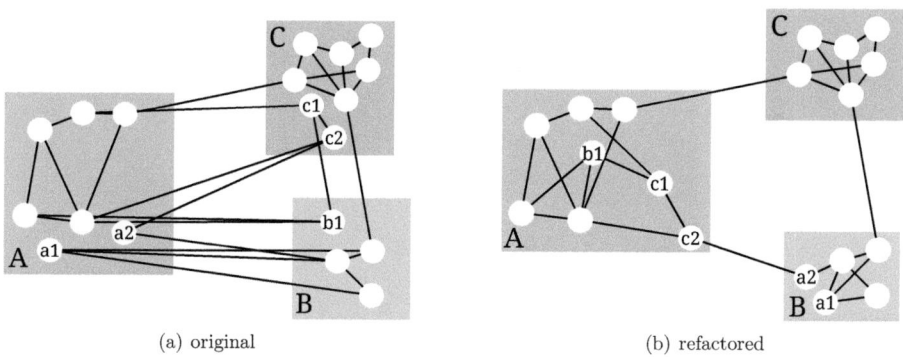

(a) original   (b) refactored

**Figure 7.2:** Illustration of move refactoring. Shaded areas represent modules, which are composed of classes (i.e. circles) bound by undirected software dependencies. Moving classes across modules can decrease the coupling between modules. (a) original modular decomposition. (b) modular decomposition after move refactoring. The resulting modules are less coupled. We emphasize that move refactoring only modifies the module membership of a class. The dependencies (i.e. links) on other classes remain untouched.

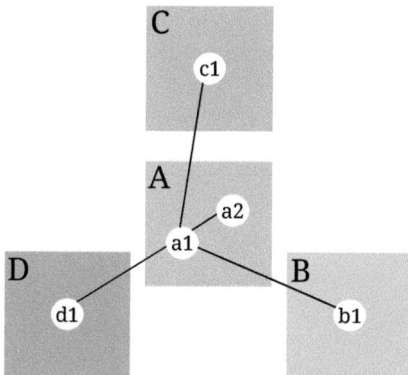

**Figure 7.3:** Class $a1$ will be refactored. It can remain in package $A$, or be moved to package $B$, $C$ or $D$. Due to the topology of this simple example (i.e. a single link to each package), each possibility has equal probability to take place. We emphasize that–using Algorithm 1–class $a1$ can only be moved to modules where it maintains software dependencies. Further generalizations are possible and will be investigated in future research.

```
initializeParameters(T, n_iterations);
network := loadNetworkFromSourceCode();
for i ← 1 to n_iterations do
    node := pickRandomNode(network);
    normTerm := 0;
    N_max := node.mostLinkedModule.numberOfLinks;
    P := emptyArray();
    for each j in modulesInNeighborhoodOf(node) do
        /*Count the number of links between node and module j*/
        N_j := countLinksToModuleJ(node.neighbors, j);
        /*The probability to move node to module j.*/
        /*The temperature parameter T controls the likelihood of bad moves.*/
        p := exp - (N_max - N_j)/T;
        normTerm := normTerm + p;
        P.append((p, j));
    end
    /*Normalize the probability distribution P*/
    for j ← 1 to P.length() do
        P[j].p := P[j].p/normTerm;
    end
    /*Decide which module receives node according to probability distribution P*/
    node.module := moveRefactoring(node, P);
    network := updateNetwork(node, network);
end
```
**Algorithm 1**: Stochastic move refactoring algorithm. The temperature parameter $T$ is a constant, therefore a cooling schedule is not required. We emphasize that a node can only be move refactored to adjacent modules in which it maintains software dependencies.

inside of the software: the more interdependent particular groups of classes are, the more likely they will be assigned–in equilibrium–to the same module.

There are several properties of this system which made it the objective of a large body of literature in the realm of physics. Here, we will simply mention a few properties that are sufficient to understand the relevance of using this model within the context of this chapter.

For the $n$-state *Potts Model*, it is possible to write for each node an individual *objective function*, which dictates the score of the current configuration of package assignment. Let $\pi_c$ denote the package a class $c$ is assigned to. Then, the objective function for class $c$ reads

$$u_c = - \sum_{c' \in \mathcal{N}(c)} \delta(\pi_c, \pi_{c'}).$$

## 7.2. METHODS

The Kronecker delta function $\delta$ is equal to one if both arguments are equal (i.e. if classes $c$ and $c'$ belong to the same package), zero, otherwise. The sum runs over all classes $c'$ which have dependency relations with class $c$, i.e. the neighborhood of $c$, represented by $\mathcal{N}(c)$. Summing up over all the nodes, we obtain

$$U = \sum_{c=1}^{k} u_c = -\sum_{c=1}^{k} \sum_{c' \in \mathcal{N}(c)} \delta(\pi_c, \pi_{c'}), \qquad (7.3)$$

which measures the total score of the current configuration. Interestingly, when class $c$ is moved from package $\pi_c$ to another $\pi'_c$, it is very simple to show that the total change is $\Delta U(\pi_c \rightarrow \pi'_c) = 2\Delta u_c$. This implies that the *local* maximization procedure, is equivalent to the *global* maximization. For this particular problem, this is a very important property, as it implies that this simple local rule is equivalent to a global one. This also implies that $U$ in Eq. 7.3 is the *total energy* of the system.

During the simulations, at every time step there are many possible configurations of module assignment for every node in the source code of the project. Over time, the algorithm *samples* the space of all possible assignments, such that the sampling probability of a given configuration is a function of Equation 7.3. The process of sampling is thus equivalent to the *Metropolis* algorithm [140], which also allows the convergence time to be determined in a standard way [49, 94, 146]. Because of the results shown in section 7.3, it is apparent that the energy landscape is not rugged, but smooth. Thereby, the modularization process proposed in this chapter always converges to a stationary state, and a simulated annealing approach (meaning the cooling schedule for the temperature) is not needed.

### 7.2.4 An Alternative Metric for Coupling and Cohesion

We follow the progress of our automated move refactoring strategy by applying the Newman's $Q$ measure, a quantitative approach widely used in complex networks theory [150, 153]. This was introduced in Chapter 6 (i.e. and in [242]) as an alternative mean to monitor the evolution of software modularity. In that empirical study, we focus on JAVA open source projects and show that $Q$ successfully expresses the congruence of the clusters of software dependencies between classes and the decomposition of source code in terms of JAVA packages. Its mathematical definition is presented in Eq. 6.1. As an illustration of its application, $Q = 0.37$ for the network in Figure 7.2(a), while $Q = 0.84$ for the one in Figure 7.2(b).

### 7.2.5 SOMOMOTO: An Eclipse Plugin for ReModularization

SOMOMOTO is an ECLIPSE plug-in and its name stands for "software modularization and monitoring tool". Its initial goal is providing a framework for remodularization of software written in JAVA. It is a tool that developers can use to monitor the evolution of a modular software architecture, both quantitatively and visually. For the quantitative part, we implement $Q$ as described in section 7.2.4, and we are planning to include other approaches available in the literature. For the visualization of modular software architectures, we make use of GEPHI's library for graph and network layout [17]. Besides monitoring software modularity, we are also able to act against its deterioration. This is achieved by implementing our automated strategy discussed in section 7.2.3. Furthermore, we plan to include competing approaches to foster direct comparison with our methodology. We also plan to allow developers to interfere with the algorithm's behavior, for example, by enabling manual move refactoring aided by an interactive network visualization. Moreover, we plan to allow the developers to define binding constraints to forbid or prioritize specific move refactoring options, to which any automated approach must comply. The source code, freely distribute with a GPL V3 license, is available at http://sourceforge.net/projects/somomoto/.

## 7.3 Results

In the following, we apply our strategy to the JAVA OSS datasets described in section 7.2.1. For each project listed in Table 7.1, we follow the procedure outlined in section 7.2.2 to extract the software dependency network of its last snapshot. This network is used as the input of our strategy (see Algorithm 1) and we run it for 20 different values for the temperature parameter $T$. We choose $T \in [0.01, 1000]$ such that these values are uniformly distributed on a logarithmic scale. We repeat this process 20 times in order to average the dynamics with respect to $T$.

### 7.3.1 The Temperature and the Equilibrium Configuration

In Figure 7.4 and 7.5, we depict the $Q$ value and the number of modules with respect to the iterations executed by our strategy. We show three projects belonging to the QUALITAS CORPUS dataset: the IDE ECLIPSE_SDK, the graphical library JUNG and the database interface HIBERNATE, because the results obtained for these three projects are representative for the projects listed in Table 7.1. In accordance with the theoretical discussion

## 7.3. RESULTS

presented in section 7.2.3, low temperature values (i.e. $T < 0.1$) lead to equilibrium configurations with low inter-module coupling and high intra-module cohesion. This range of temperature makes deteriorating move refactoring steps very unlikely. Thus software modularity improves substantially, as expressed in terms of the high $Q$ values seen in figures 7.4(a), 7.4(b) and 7.4(c).

Interestingly, the highest $Q$ values and the lowest number of modules are obtained within an intermediate temperature range (i.e. $0.1 < T < 10$). For this range, we show in Table 7.2 that a small improvement in $Q$ (i.e. $\approx 4.0\%$)–with respect to the range $T < 0.1$– is associated with a comparably larger drop in the number of modules (i.e. $\approx 17\%$). Furthermore, as depicted in Figures 7.5(a), 7.5(b) and 7.5(c), the execution of our strategy always leads to a significant drop in the number of modules. For the lowest temperature (i.e. $T = 0.01$) this drop is lowest and corresponds to losing $68.4 \pm 13.2\%$ of the original modules. For higher temperatures, the drop is even larger. Thus, as a side effect of our strategy, a substantial fraction of the original structure of the source code is lost. Although associated with an improvement in modularity, it is not understood how this drop in the number of modules can affect development performance. More research is needed to study if for example, this extra improvement of $\approx 4\%$ in $Q$ values (e.g. from 166% to 170%) justify a further drop of 17% in the number of modules (e.g. from 68% to 85%). As a rule of thumb–if remodularization is expected to preserve the most possible of the original modular structure–only values of $T \ll 0.1$ should be considered.

**Table 7.2:** Average values for the change in $Q$ and in the number of modules for different temperature ranges. For the lowest temperature (i.e. $T = 0.01$) our strategy improves $Q$ in $166.6 \pm 77.3\%$, while decreasing the number of modules in $68.4 \pm 13.2\%$.

| Temperature Range | $\Delta Q$ (%) | $\Delta$ Modules (%) |
|---|---|---|
| $T = 0.01$ (lowest) | $166.6 \pm 77.3$ | $-68.4 \pm 13.2$ |
| $T < 0.1$ | $166.5 \pm 77.6$ | $-68.4 \pm 13.2$ |
| $0.1 < T < 10$ | $170.5 \pm 105.2$ | $-85.4 \pm 9.7$ |
| $10 < T$ | $-50.1 \pm 18.6$ | $-82.9 \pm 9.7$ |
| $T = 1000$ (highest) | $-52.1 \pm 16.7$ | $-82.4 \pm 9.9$ |

Figure 7.6(a) depicts the relation between $Q$ and the number of modules on the temperature parameter $T$. In this figure, we only consider the equilibrium values of the former two quantities. We bin the data points with respect to $T$ and calculate the median value. We also show the 90% and 10% quantiles. The first insight is that the variability in $Q$ is almost constant with respect to $T$, decreasing slightly during the abrupt change between high and low $Q$ values. For small $T$, the variability in the number of modules is comparably higher, but decreases significantly as $T$ increases. Another insight is the abrupt change

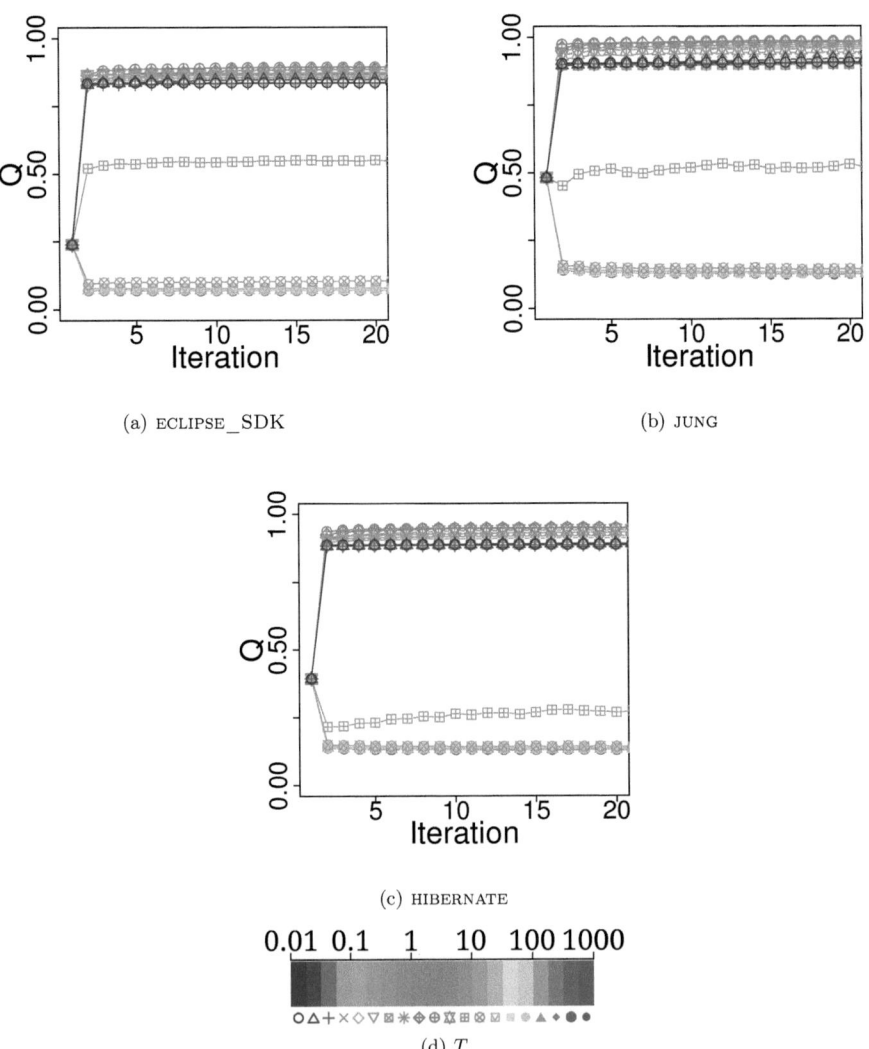

**Figure 7.4:** Evolution of $Q$ during move refactoring steps. The iteration number $k$ displayed in the horizontal axis of each figure corresponds to $100 \times m \times k$ move refactoring steps (i.e. $m$ being the number of JAVA classes). Each curve represents the average of 20 runs of our strategy with different values of the temperature parameter $T$.

## 7.3. RESULTS

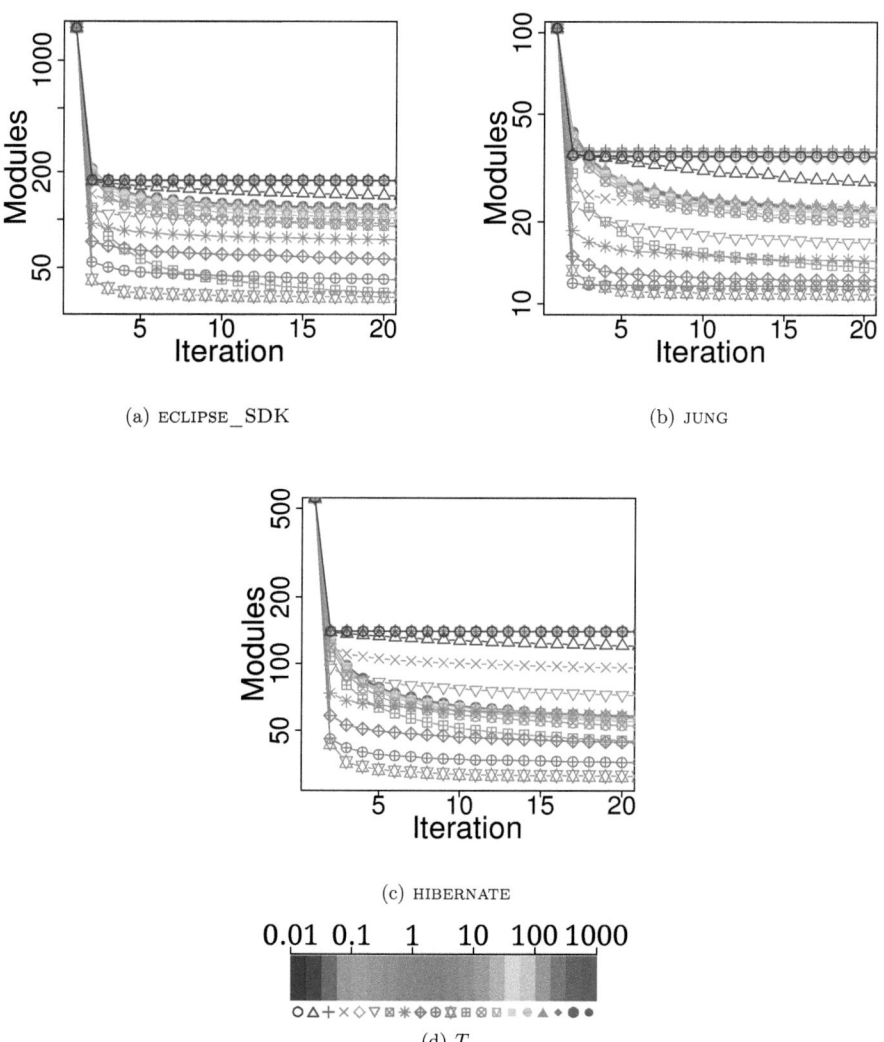

**Figure 7.5:** Evolution of the number of required modules (i.e. non-empty modules) during move refactoring steps. For intermediary values (i.e. $0.1 < T < 10$) we obtain the highest $Q$ values on the expense of losing a significant fraction of the original modules. Thus, the use of $T < 0.1$ is recommended (see Figure 7.4).

in $Q$ about $T = 10$. For $T < 10$ we observe values of $Q$ which are significantly higher than for $T > 10$. This is further illustrated in Figure 7.6(b), which depicts the potential energy difference between these two states: high potential energy (i.e. high modularity and high $Q$) and low potential energy (i.e. low modularity and low $Q$). As a final remark, these two contrasting potential energy levels are the reason why we only observe few equilibrium states in figures 7.4(a), 7.4(b) and 7.4(c): high $Q$ (i.e. high potential energy), intermediary $Q$ (i.e. transitional state) and low $Q$ (i.e. low potential energy).

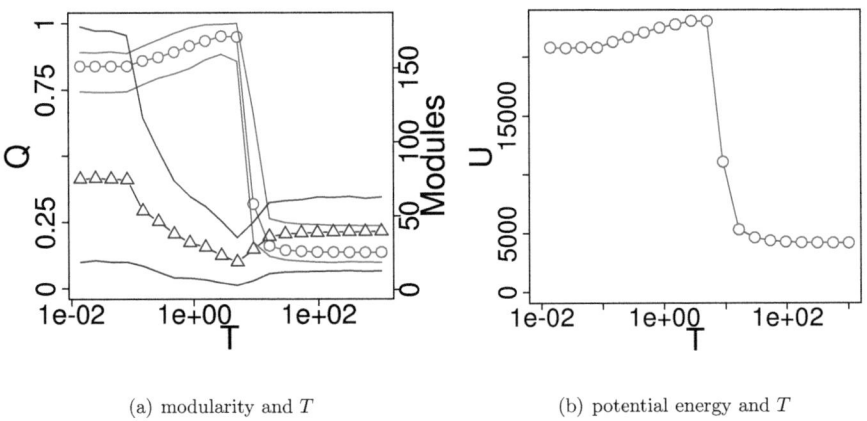

(a) modularity and $T$  (b) potential energy and $T$

**Figure 7.6:** The role of the temperature $T$ as a control parameter. (a) Dependency of $Q$ (i.e. dashed red circles) and the number of required modules (i.e. dashed blue triangles) with the temperature $T$. Each curve is obtained by measuring the median value of the corresponding measures, when considering the simulation results aggregated over $T$. The solid curves above and below the corresponding measure represent the 90.0% and 10.0% quantiles respectively. There is an abrupt change in the value of $Q$ as a function of the control parameter $T$. (b) Median value of the corresponding potential energy $U$. Structured or well modularized software falls into the $T$ range mapping to a higher potential energy level (i.e. $T < 10$), while poorly structured software falls into the deep valley with low potential energy level (i.e. $T > 10$).

## 7.3. RESULTS

### 7.3.2 Remodularization Performance of our Strategy

In Figure 7.7(a), we show that the performance of our strategy does not depend on the number of modules (i.e. no correlation between $Q$ and the number of modules). Furthermore, our strategy improved the modularity of all projects considered in this chapter, resulting in remodularized software with an average value of $Q = 0.8 \pm 0.1$ for $T = 0.01$. Finally, the worse the modularity of a given architecture, the higher the relative improvement as a result of the application of our strategy. We depict this in Figure 7.7(b). Further research will investigate if these results hold for different datasets.

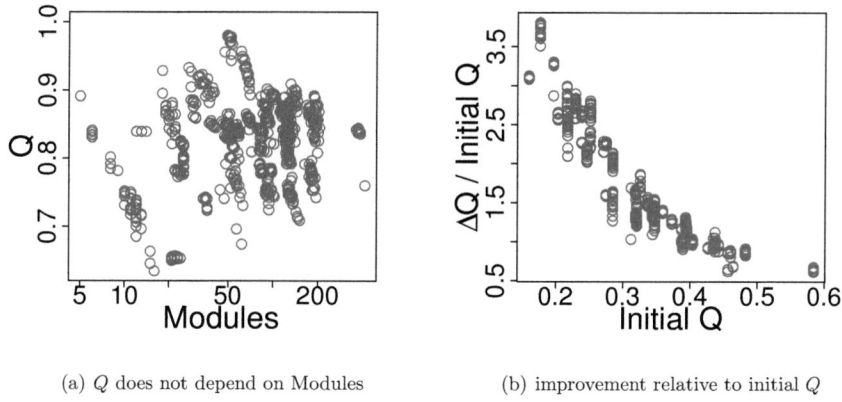

(a) $Q$ does not depend on Modules

(b) improvement relative to initial $Q$

**Figure 7.7:** The performance of our strategy at equilibrium with $T = 0.01$. (a) In the studied dataset, the number of modules does not correlate with $Q$, thus we can discard any dependency of this kind. (b) The worse the initial value of $Q$ (i.e. the worse the initial modular design), the larger the improvement achieved.

### 7.3.3 Move Refactoring in Empirical Data

In this section, we verify if the move refactoring suggestions discovered by our strategy were actually executed in empirical data. We focus on the CVS logs dataset, which reflects the iterative development process with greater regularity, following closely the coding decisions undertaken by the software developers.

In order to perform this comparison, we first need to be able to detect move refactoring taking place within our datasets. We solve this problem in the following way. We define a time stamped CVS log snapshot $s_t$, which corresponds to the set of class dependencies and respective package (module) membership observed at time $t$. Each class in $s_t$ is named with respect to the pattern *package_name$_t$.class_name$_t$*. To detect move refactoring, we take the simple approach of looking for unique class names (*class_name$_t$*) in $s_t$, verifying if these names are found in $s_{t+1}$. If the answer is positive, we check for modifications in the respective package names (*package_name$_t$*). Thus, move refactoring is detected when *class_name$_t$* = *class_name$_{t+1}$* and *package_name$_t$* $\neq$ *package_name$_{t+1}$*. We emphasize that this approach only detects move refactoring of the kind defined in this chapter: a refactoring step that only modifies the package membership of a class, without touching upon any of its contents and the network of software dependencies.

With the move refactoring detection method outlined above, we are able to compare our strategy output with the work of the software developers. For each two consecutive CVS log snapshot $s_t$ and $s_{t+1}$, we extract the respective empirical software dependency networks $net_t^e$ and $net_{t+1}^e$ (see section 7.2.2). Let $D$ be the set of move refactoring steps performed by the developers between $net_t^e$ and $net_{t+1}^e$. Furthermore, we use $net_t^e$ as the input of our algorithm and let it run until convergence (for $T = 0.01$). The network of software dependencies resulting from this procedure is defined as $net_{t+1}^s$. Finally, let $S$ be the set of move refactoring steps performed by our strategy and detected between $net_t^e$ and $net_{t+1}^s$. We compare these two sets, thresholding on the $\Delta Q$ between $t$ and $t+1$, so that we focus on move refactoring taking place during significant improvements in software modularity. For different values of $\Delta Q$, we calculate *precision* and *recall* and present the results in Table 7.3. The results show that our strategy correctly suggest most of the move refactoring steps performed by the software developers, as indicated by the relatively high values listed in the column *recall*. In fact, our algorithm is much more *aggressive*[3] than the developers when suggesting move refactoring steps. Thus, our resulting set of suggestions is much larger than the set chosen by developers. This is the reason why our *precision* values are relatively small: the software developers do not use move refactoring consistently as mean to restore software modularity.

### 7.3.4 SOMOMOTO in Action

As a simple test case, we employ SOMOMOTO in the remodularization of a JAVA graphical library called JGRAPHX. Figure 7.8 depicts the software dependency network and

---

[3] we further discuss this in section 7.4

## 7.4. THREATS TO VALIDITY

**Table 7.3:** Comparison between the set of move refactoring steps suggested by our strategy $S$, against the set of steps performed by the developers $D$ upon the empirical data. Quantitatively: $precision = \frac{|S \cap D|}{|S|}$ and $recall = \frac{|S \cap D|}{|D|}$. We present these measures for different values of the threshold parameter $\Delta Q$ (i.e. change in modularity measured in empirical data), thus allowing us to focus on the move refactoring steps that had significant impact on software modularity.

| $\Delta Q$ (%) | $precision$ (%) | $recall$ (%) |
|---|---|---|
| 1 | $4.9 \pm 15.7$ | $59.9 \pm 35.4$ |
| 5 | $7.0 \pm 16.9$ | $62.4 \pm 35.3$ |
| 10 | $8.1 \pm 19.2$ | $62.7 \pm 39.0$ |
| 15 | $5.7 \pm 8.9$ | $52.4 \pm 40.8$ |

the module membership of classes of JGRAPX, before and after remodularization. The resulting network, depicted in Figure 7.8(b), clearly shows the congruence between the clusters of software dependencies and the source code decomposition into JAVA packages. Network nodes (i.e. classes) bearing the same color are members of the same modules (i.e. packages).

## 7.4 Threats to Validity

Here, we address some of the concerns related to the results of our approach. The first issue is our conscious decision of not considering the semantics of modules during the remodularization via automated move refactorings. We are well aware of the fact that there are modules whose contents should not be move refactored, in despite of their significant impact on inter-module coupling. For example, modules responsible for user interfaces may fall within this category. Related to this issue, there might be modules that are believed to be already well structured. In such cases, further refactoring them would be detrimental. The simplest solution, which we are planning to include in SOMOMOTO, is to allow developers to mark modules and also classes that should not be remodularized by an automated refactoring strategy. Further ideas related to direct interference in the behavior of the algorithm, allowing it to cope with developer preferences are possible. For example, the contents of obsolete modules might need to be move refactored into other modules. For such cases, our strategy can be applied by focusing on a few modules, redistributing their content.

Another issue that might be circumvented by allowing the direct interference of software developers is the observed significant drop in the number of modules, even for small values

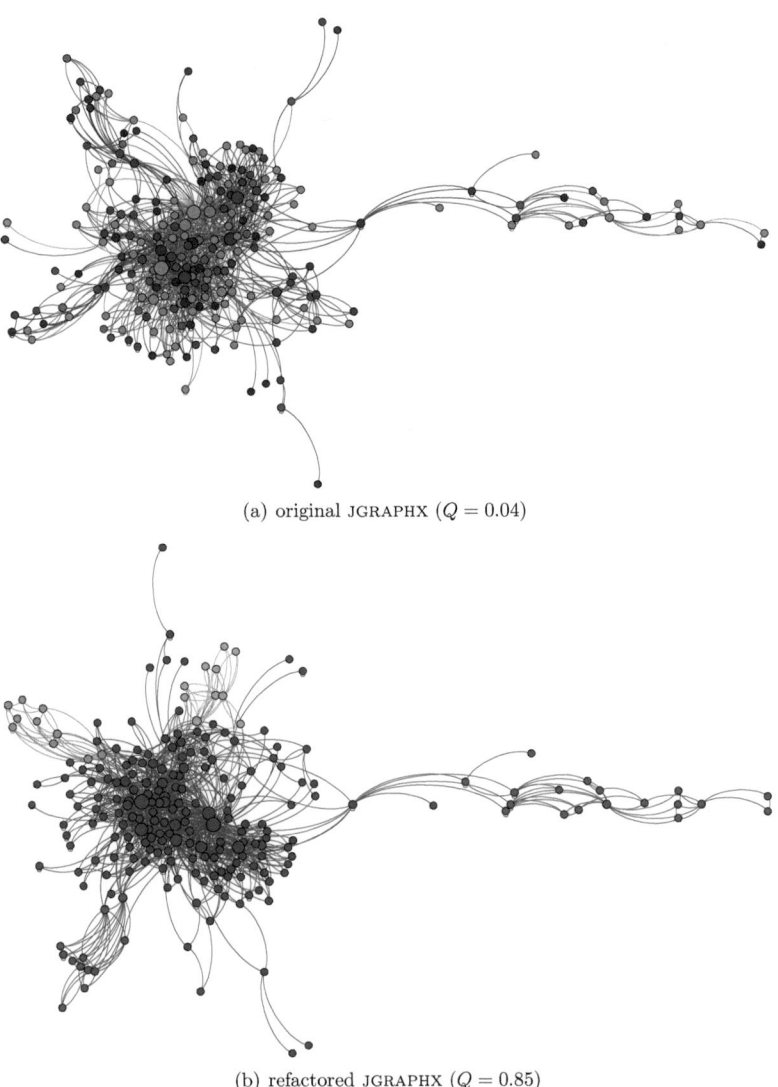

(a) original JGRAPHX ($Q = 0.04$)

(b) refactored JGRAPHX ($Q = 0.85$)

**Figure 7.8:** Test case: the remodularization of JGRAPHX (a JAVA graphical library). The JAVA classes are depicted as circles, while their color reflects the corresponding package membership (same color, same package). (a) original. (b) after remodularization by SOMOMOTO.

of the temperature parameter $T$. Our results show that at least $\approx 68\%$ become empty. One possible explanation is found in [19], where the authors study a similar dataset of JAVA OSS projects, showing that the minimization of the inter-module coupling and maximization of intra-module cohesion is not a dominating module design principle. Thus, a more realistic perspective on automated remodularization should include complementary quantitative dimensions. These additions, together with the implementation of competing approaches, will be included in our ECLIPSE plug-in, in order to foster direct comparison with our methodology, and also to provide a unified framework for the remodularization of JAVA software. These steps will foster its use in practice. We are further interested in the opinion of software developers on the outcome of our automated move refactoring strategy, also to understand if the seldom use of move refactoring observed in our datasets is a general issue. We expect that move refactoring, based on our automated strategy, will be more frequently applied in practice. As shown in this chapter, the underlying problem landscape seems to be smooth, at least with respect to the temperature parameter $T$. Thus, a convergence to favorable software modularities can be ensured.

## 7.5 Related Work

Software evolves in ways that do not necessarily reflect positively in its modularity. In order to cope with the deterioration of the latter, refactoring strategies can be employed. It has been argued in [34, 64], that approaches considering developer expertise–to directly refactor the source code–seldom allow for a significant improvement in software modularity. The difficulties are mainly related to the problem of detecting possible candidates for refactoring. This opens up many opportunities for the development of automated refactoring methodologies. Among the available approaches, the ones that imply a reformulation of software modularity as a combinatorial problem are quite common. Furthermore, most of those are mainly concerned with the minimization of inter-module coupling and maximization of intra-module cohesion [8], as dictated by software engineering wisdom [61, 159, 199], both have potentially high impact on maintenance costs. One of the earliest approaches in this direction offers an optimization search guided by a genetic algorithm [62]. Their search starts with an initial modular decomposition, which at each iteration is replaced by the best decomposition found in a population controlled by the algorithm. A simple variation of this approach is to allow multiple searches to take place in parallel, such that a majority rule is used to determine the best modular decomposition [135]. An alternative way to escape local optima is discussed in [1]. Similar to our own approach, they apply simulated annealing allowing the acceptance of moves that do not always improve the functional being maximized. Moves that improve the respective functional are always accepted. Our approach is different for being completely governed by Eq. 7.1, such that every move bears a probability of being executed. Their absolute contribution to the energy function influences this probability but do not force an immediate acceptance. The authors also introduce constraints to limit some aspects of the optimization search that are missing here: maximal number of classes that can change their packages, maximal number of classes that a package can contain and the classes that should not change their packages. These are in line with the idea of having software developers interfering with automated approaches more effectively, as discussed in [125, 161]. We plan to include this methodology in future releases of our plug-in. Furthermore, [1] report results on modularity improvement only for highly limited values for these three constraints. These result in small improvement in modularity, which cannot be compared to the results–significantly higher–that we present in our work. Complementary to the discussion above, the work presented in [19] classifies modules by their role within the architecture. They show that modules controlling *io* and *gui* functions are the most congruent regarding cohesion and coupling metrics. Moreover, [18, 167] advocate the use of metrics based on the semantics of modules besides structural dependencies. According to [85, 86], structural dependencies are not uniformly important with respect to the propagation of changes. Thus they emphasize that future research should focus on their semantics rather than the structure. Other approaches in the literature seek to group software constructs into modules according to measures that express their similarity, a technique better known as *clustering*. Examples of works within this context are presented in [9, 125, 161]. In [232], a comparison between different clustering strategies concludes that clustering algorithms do not reproduce the existing modular decomposition of software projects, calling for further research.

## 7.6 Conclusion

In conclusion, we have introduced a simple stochastic algorithm that allows to remodularize software architectures based on an automated suggestion of *move refactorings*. This algorithm is based on the assumption that an optimum modular design of software minimizes the *coupling* between modules, while the *cohesion* within modules is maximized. We take a complex networks perspective on modularity in software dependency networks and capture both cohesion and coupling by a network-based, quantitative measure. Furthermore, making use of the $n$-state *Potts Model* known from statistical physics, our stochastic algorithm provides a complex systems approach to the optimization of software modularity in dependency networks. We validate the remodularization performance of our algorithm by applying it to two datasets which allows us to study the evolution of software dependency networks for 39 JAVA open source software projects. The results of our analysis validate that the modularity of these projects can be increased on average by $166 \pm 77\%$. We further show that the achievable gain in modularity is related to the level of modularity in the initial architecture, hence indicating the presence of a significant modularization potential in architectures that exhibit low modularity. Based on empirical data on the evolution of software modularity in JAVA projects, we further extract *move refactorings* performed by developers to remodularize the software architecture. We then compare the suggestions of our algorithm with the actual actions of developers and compare *precision* and *recall* of the refactoring suggestions. The fact that our approach achieves a comparably high recall while the precision is low highlights that a) our method suggests most of the move refactorings that were identified by developers and b) that our method was able to identify many more move refactoring than were actually implemented by real developers. We argue that this finding opens a number of interesting further research directions: First, it can be seen as a challenge for the assumption that optimal modular designs (from the perspective of developers) coincide with a maximization of cohesion and a minimization of coupling. Reasons for this most likely include the importance of context in the choice of the package decomposition of projects, as well as the existence of dependencies to third-party packages whose modular structure cannot be easily changed. Secondly, it can be interpreted in such a way that our method highlights a significant modularization potential that currently goes unused in actual software projects. Finally, it highlights the necessity of introducing an additional parameter to our algorithm, that influences how *aggressive* it is. In summary, we argue that our work is a promising example for the applicability of models, methods and abstractions from the study of complex systems and complex networks in software engineering.

# Chapter 8

# Conclusions

> "My entire life consisted of musings, calculations, practical works, and trials. Many questions remain unanswered, many works are incomplete or unpublished. The most important things still lie ahead."
>
> KONSTANTIN E. TSIOLKOVSKY

## 8.1 Summary

In this thesis, we adopt a complex systems perspective to study a number of software engineering processes. More specifically, we focus on social collaborations within bug handling communities and the dynamics of software modularity. The presentation is divided into two main parts: Part I is focused on the role of social interactions while shaping social organization and knowledge sharing. Part II is focused on the impact of software dependencies on the modular decomposition of software. We argue that both share a topological structure that is suitable for the application of quantitative methods based on complex networks theory: social interactions can be aggregated into a social network, while software dependencies have an implicit network topology.

In Part I, we focus on social aspects influencing the organization of bug handling communities built around open source software projects. We apply social network analysis to quantify the dynamics of social organization of each community. We focus on the GENTOO project and report on a remarkable period of centralization with associated changes in community performance. Between 2004–2008, a contributor to whom we refer as *Alice*, became central within the community: she was responsible for the most of the bug report triaging and processing. We observe that during this period, the community performance was maximized. We confirm our quantitative findings by interviewing a number of prominent contributors related to these events, including *Alice* herself. They complement our analysis with their own account on the steps that led to the centralization, how it evolved, and the respective outcome. One of the insights provided by these interviews is that, having a single dedicated person triaging bug reports is more efficient. This minimizes coordination requirements and also fosters the identification of duplicate reports. In addition, we present insightful network visualizations that illustrate the respective changes in social organization. What is special about this centralization event is the fact that *Alice* left the community suddenly. This was also acknowledged in the interviews. The community struggled to restructure its procedures and cope with this abrupt change, the latter having a lastingly negative effect on performance. We conclude that centralization can be beneficial and risky. Thus, it is important for managers to be aware of centralization, and we argue that our methodology can be used as a quantitative mean to improve human resource management. Furthermore, we investigate the reasons that influenced *Alice* to leave the community. Our strategy was inspired by *Alice*'s own account explaining her reasons for departuring. *Alices* states that she lost motivation due to a "[...]disruptive social environment in the project as a whole[...]". As social interactions between GENTOO contributors take place online, we focus our investigation on the communication channels used by the bug handling community: the *bug tracker* and the *developers mainling list*. By processing textual messages with quantitative methods based on sentiment analysis, we are able to confirm that communication involving *Alice* was predominantly negative. Moreover, inspired by this finding, we extend our approach and study how GENTOO contributors, in general, are influenced by the emotions expressed within these channels. We observe a correlation between emotional intensity–rather than polarity–and the likelihood that these contributors will decrease their activity. We propose an automatic prediction methodology that can be used as a tool supporting management, by increasing awareness with respect to community *mood* and turnover. Thus, allowing community managers to take preemptive actions against significant turnover events. We conclude with a practical application of social network analysis as a mean to obtain automatic high accuracy bug report triaging. Often, bug reports do not lead to a positive solution improving the software. This is the case for bug reports found to be e.g. invalid, incomplete or duplicate. The issue here is that these possibilities are detected only after a significant time investment. We propose an automated strategy to allow the prioritization of bug reports that will lead to software improvement. We show that we can predict if a bug report is worth processing based on the social embeddededness of the bug reporter, at the reporting time. To do so, for each new bug report, we aggregate all social interactions taking place within the community in the previous 30 days. On this network, we compute nine measures that expresses the bug reporter's social embeddededness. We use these measures as the input of a machine learning tool that automatically classifies the bug report as *valid* or *invalid*. We obtain remarkable high accuracy, and we emphasize that this only considers social network analysis at the reporting time. Thus, our methodology bears great practical relevance.

Finally, in Part II we study the dynamics of software modularity. We argue that having a well structured modular architecture fosters its maintainability and expandability. We use quantitative methods from complex networks theory, namely Newman's $Q$ modularity, to investigate the congruence between the clusters of software dependencies and the decomposition of the source code into modules. The more the software dependencies match the modular decomposition, the higher the $Q$ value. We observe, in an empirical analysis considering the source code of JAVA open source software projects, that modularity can deteriorate over time. Thus, we propose a methodology based on a stochastic algorithm that can be used to restore software modularity. Our strategy is based on a well known restructuring approach named *refactoring*. We test our method in an empirical study, and interpret its dynamics in terms of statistical physics concepts. We show that our method always improve software modularity, and that its gain is higher for poorly modularized software. Thus, the worse the software, the better the improvement after our approach.

With the examples presented in this thesis, we show how software engineering research and practice can benefit from complex systems theory. We argue that many more software engineering processes are intrinsically complex, and should be studied as such: complexity cannot be reduced or ignored. On the contrary, we show that complexity can be quantified and can be applied to obtain meaningful results. The remaining of this concluding chapter is organized as follows. In section 8.2 we discuss the implications of our contributions upon different scientific fields, and we conclude in section 8.3 by discussing further research directions and open questions.

## 8.2 Scientific Scope

Due to the interdisciplinarity of our research, the contributions of this thesis have implications that touch upon several knowledge domains. Thus, we take a step back and interpret our findings under these different perspectives. In the following, we focus on what we believe to be the domains upon which our research will have the most impact.

### 8.2.1 Social Organization & Management

Is it possible to understand social organization to a level in which we can actually interfere with its dynamics, steering it towards high efficiency and high performance? A positive answer to this question implies that we are able to meaningfully apply quantitative approaches. As correctly expressed in [174], "[...]you can't control what you can't measure[...]". Traditionally, the study of social organizations is a field that relies strongly on qualitative methods [35, 89, 155, 179], and is increasingly being complemented by different quantitative frameworks, especially when focusing on the role of social ties influencing other processes [42, 123, 157, 188, 200]. Our research contributes to this effort, by providing in Chapter 2 a complementary dynamic perspective on social network analysis. We show that we can closely follow changes in social organization by keeping track of measures that quantify the social embeddedness of individuals and community cohesion.

In Chapter 3 this methodology allowed us to document the rise and fall of a central contributor (named *Alice*) within the bug handling community of the GENTOO project. An interesting finding on its own, as it bears special relevance for the management literature on *star performers* [88, 177]. We observe that *Alice*'s trajectory was positively influenced by her outstanding dedication to the project, thus in line with the literature [92, 108]. However, the mechanism by which *Alice* became central was also responsible for increasing the *tension* between her and other contributors [2], leading to *Alices*'s sudden departure from GENTOO: she was intermediating most of the communication within the community. As *Alice* explains, she attributes her departure from GENTOO by claiming that the project had a "[...]disruptive social environment[...]". Indeed, the communication channels in which *Alice* was active had a predominant *negative tone*. We confirm that with a quantitative method based on sentiment analysis presented in Chapter 4.

Interestingly, *Alice*'s sudden departure was felt quickly by the community, as open issues accumulated fast: there was a high dependence on *Alice*'s dedication. To cope with *Alice*'s absence, dramatic changes were orchestrated by community managers in order to restructure their procedures. According to the literature, this collective struggle could be the result of a fast increase with respect to *sense of community* within the GENTOO project [138, 175]. As defined in [180], sense of community refers to "[...]the perception of similarity to others, an acknowledged interdependence with others, a willingness to maintain this interdependence by giving to or doing for others what one expects from them, and the feeling that one is part of a larger dependable and stable structure[...]".

Finally, we also study the factors that influence the success of individuals within a social organization [45, 95, 203]. We illustrate this by showing how we can prioritize bug reports, based on the social embeddedness of the respective authors. Our results show that success is determined by a number of factors expressing position within the social network. Among the possible explanatory mechanisms, direct and indirect *knowledge spillovers* are very plausible [71]. The literature acknowledges that embeddedness (networking) increases the fitness of individual nodes (e.g. contributors, projects, firms, etc) but argues that there might be a threshold after which the network effects of embeddedness are detrimental [215]. In general, estimating the relevance of each determining factor with respect to the phenomenon is a science on its own [102]. However, when a practical application–such as prediction–is required, we do not need to interpret each factor in isolation. As we show in Chapter 5, machine learning techniques can handle these multidimensional factors and produce high accuracy results.

To summarize, we discuss a number of quantitative methods that bear great relevance to management and social organization practice and research. Moreover, as we illustrate in this section, research in the social sciences can use data generated by open source communities to study problems of broader relevance, i.e. not limited to software engineering and its subdomains.

## 8.2.2 Computer Science

It is remarkable that we can ignore the contents of a bug report in favor of a social network, to decide if the bug report is *valid* (will lead to a fix) or *invalid* (e.g. duplicate, incomplete, etc). Arguably, Chapter 5 presents the most striking contribution of this thesis. This result is a combination of two ingredients: *machine learning techniques* and *the role and dynamics of social ties*. Is this finding an isolated case? That means, predicting the quality of a technical artifact based on social embeddedness. Can it be reframed and generalized to different problems? If this answer is positive, will we need a new framework to study how computers can learn from society (*computational social learning theory*) [14]? Currently and in a broader perspective, this is addressed by the field of *socio-technical systems* [213, 228]. These correspond to systems that are characterized by a strong dependence on the collective dynamics of a social counterpart: distributed systems [182], networks [38], traffic [105], online behavior [163], search engines [15] are all influenced by the interaction between the people that use their infrastructure. Thus, to design efficient social-technical systems, engineers must take complexity into account. For example, *organic computing* is one of the promising approaches originated within the computer science context [141, 182].

As a conclusion, in this thesis we show how we tune a social-technical systems in order to foster an increase in its productivity. We apply a *social information filtering* scheme [192] that allows the community to prioritize tasks and improve resource management. Thus, our results provide inspiring examples on how complexity can be handled by computer science efficiently.

### 8.2.3 Physics of Complex Networks

We argue that open source data is of great value for the study of *temporal networks*. These online communities are very active and regularly generate large volumes of time-stamped data. Thus, the examples presented in this thesis should stand as and inspiration for new discoveries.

Complex networks theory documents a wide range of measures that quantify the structural properties of network topologies. Often, the main focus is on node centrality [152]. These measures, however, have mostly been developed and applied to static, time-independent networks (aggregated networks). This framework is accurate enough for the results presented in Part II, which is only concerned with static networks of software dependencies. However, when focusing on social interactions, the meaning of links will depend on the time scale of the aggregation. The longer this time scale, the more static the resulting network will be. In Part I, we show how to use sliding time windows to study the dynamics of social interactions, using an intermediary level of aggregation. Although limited, this approach yields important results, but we emphasize that there is a general lack in terms of a framework to deal with the instantaneous dynamics of link formation. New developments in the literature of temporal networks demonstrate that the link aggregation can produce misleading network topologies [164, 183]. The latter is the result of paths that are not realizable with respect to the original time sequencing of the links. They advocate that time needs to be taken into account, and that this can be done with suitable quantitative methods [164]. In this thesis, we present many examples depicting the dynamics of social interactions. We show plots presenting the changes in social organization within several open source communities. Furthermore, in Chapter 5, we described statistical results showing that the centrality of individuals reporting *duplicate* bug reports decrease after the reporting time (see Table 5.2). We discuss several hypothesis related to these findings. We argue that only a framework based on temporal networks will lead to more precise explanations. Finally, the social networks studied in this thesis are only *one-mode*[1] projections of *two-mode* networks[2]. We argue that further improvements and complementary insights can be obtained by using a framework that addresses the latter [43, 194].

---
[1]interactions between contributors
[2]composed of two kinds of nodes (*bugs* and *contributors*)

## 8.3 Outlook and Concluding Thoughts

Science is a problem generating enterprise. Every time we try to answer a research question, it is likely that we find other questions. Therefore, rather than providing the ultimate answer that closes a research line, we end up opening new research lines. So does this thesis. In section 8.2, we outline research lines derived from the interdisciplinarity of our resutls. In this section, we conclude our work by discussing further ideas of relevance to software engineering and its complexity.

Can we generalize our results with respect to software engineering at large? The main issue here is that all of our datasets were generated by open source software projects. As stated in the, by now famous[3], *Linus Law*, "given enough eye balls, all bugs are shallow" [170]. Skeptics state that having enough contributors[1] does not imply that all bugs will be discovered and corrected [90]. However, taking a different perspective, we argue here that it is only by enabling access to the source code that contributors of software projects can express their full capability and skill in all possible dimensions [223]. We argue that the results presented in Part I are valid with respect to any online community, when the goal is the quantification of the dynamics of social organization. However, it is not known to which extent "closed" source software hinders the ability of contributors to interact with each other online, a crucial ingredient of our approach to the automatic categorization of bug reports based on social network analysis. Rephrasing our starting question: *When* can we generalize our results with respect to software engineering at large? Interestingly enough, it is a matter of time. Global software engineering industry and practice are becoming, in many ways, more and more like open source projects: e.g. distributed development, number of contributors, geographic dispersion of teams, community-base issue tracking, etc [12, 22, 101, 106, 129, 136, 148, 205]. As for the results presented in Part II, we argue that there are no major conflicts: our methodology can be employed in any software project.

Furthermore, software engineering literature contains lengthy discussions about issues related to the *technical debit*. The latter is a metaphor describing a software maintenance dichotomy: the *quick and dirty* approach, which is easy to implement, but hard to modify in the future, and the *well structured and clean* approach, that takes longer to implement and requires major refactoring [33, 52]. The metaphor comes from finance, where the equivalent of *quick and dirty* is the payment of an interest rate due to a debit that cannot be cleared. We argue that the *social debit*–the social counterpart of technical debit–deserves the same attention [204]. This will influence how we perceive community

---

[3]*Linus Law* and our definition for *contributor* are discussed in Chapter 2

building [198, 226] and its resilience [81, 134]. For example, in the case study reported in Chapter 3, we observe the rise and fall of *Alice* within the GENTOO community. Clearly, the choice of this community was the *quick and dirty*, as it passively allowed *Alice* to concentrate most of the work load on herself. Although it was very convenient for the community to rely mainly on a single contributor, we argue in Chapter 3 that this was a risky approach. Indeed, after *Alice*'s sudden departure, the community had no choice but to start major changes [115, 197].

Finally, the literature on software engineering is converging towards a framework unifying social and technical aspects of software development, the so called *socio-technical congruence* [27, 28, 29, 36, 37, 128, 216, 217]. In general terms, they argue that dependencies between technical problems must match the dependencies between social coordination efforts. To test this claim, the literature is developing quantitative methods which admit the use of approaches based on complex networks theory, thus generating new opportunities for the application of the results presented in this thesis.

# Bibliography

[1] Abdeen, H.; Ducasse, S.; Sahraoui, H.; Alloui, I. (2009). Automatic package coupling and cycle minimization. In: *Reverse Engineering, 2009. WCRE'09. 16th Working Conference on.* IEEE, pp. 103–112.

[2] Adler, G. (1997). When your star performer can't manage. *Harvard business review* **75(4)**, 22.

[3] Ahmadi, N.; Jazayeri, M.; Lelli, F.; Nesic, S. (2008). A survey of social software engineering. In: *Automated Software Engineering-Workshops, 2008. ASE Workshops 2008. 23rd IEEE/ACM International Conference on.* IEEE, pp. 1–12.

[4] Albert, R.; Barabási, A.-L. (2002). Statistical mechanics of complex networks. *Reviews of modern physics* **74(1)**, 47.

[5] Ancona, D.; Zucca, E. (2001). True modules for Java-like languages. In: *ECOOP 2001—Object-Oriented Programming*, Springer. pp. 354–380.

[6] Anderson, P. W.; *et al.* (1972). More is different. *Science* **177(4047)**, 393–396.

[7] Andreoni, J. (1990). Impure Altruism and Donations to Public Goods: A Theory of Warm-Glow Giving. *The Economic Journal* **100(401)**, 464.

[8] Anquetil, N.; Laval, J. (2011). Legacy software restructuring: Analyzing a concrete case. In: *Software Maintenance and Reengineering (CSMR), 2011 15th European Conference on.* IEEE, pp. 279–286.

[9] Antoniol, G.; Di Penta, M.; Neteler, M. (2003). Moving to smaller libraries via clustering and genetic algorithms. In: *Software Maintenance and Reengineering, 2003. Proceedings. Seventh European Conference on.* IEEE, pp. 307–316.

[10] Anvik, J. (2006). Automating bug report assignment. In: *Proceedings of the 28th international conference on Software engineering.* ICSE '06, ACM, pp. 937–940.

[11] Arthur, W. B. (1999). Complexity and the economy. *science* **284(5411)**, 107–109.

[12] Babar, M. A.; Zahedi, M. (2013). Understanding Structures and Affordances of Extended Teams in Global Software Development. In: *Global Software Engineering (ICGSE), 2013 IEEE 8th International Conference on*. IEEE, pp. 226–235.

[13] Backstrom, L.; Huttenlocher, D.; Kleinberg, J.; Lan, X. (2006). Group formation in large social networks. In: *Proceedings of the 12th international conference on Knowledge discovery and data mining - KDD '06*. p. 44.

[14] Bandura, A.; McClelland, D. C. (1977). *Social learning theory*. Prentice-Hall Englewood Cliffs, NJ.

[15] Bar-Ilan, J.; Mat-Hassan, M.; Levene, M. (2006). Methods for comparing rankings of search engine results. *Computer Networks* **50(10)**, 1448–1463.

[16] Barabasi, A.-L. (2005). The origin of bursts and heavy tails in human dynamics. *Nature* **435(7039)**, 207–11.

[17] Bastian, M.; Heymann, S.; Jacomy, M. (2009). Gephi: An Open Source Software for Exploring and Manipulating Networks. In: *Proceedings of the ICWSM '09*. AAAI.

[18] Bavota, G.; De Lucia, A.; Marcus, A.; Oliveto, R. (2010). Software re-modularization based on structural and semantic metrics. In: *Reverse Engineering (WCRE), 2010 17th Working Conference on*. IEEE, pp. 195–204.

[19] Beck, F.; Diehl, S. (2011). On the congruence of modularity and code coupling. In: *Proceedings of the 19th ACM SIGSOFT symposium and the 13th European conference on Foundations of software engineering*. ACM, pp. 354–364.

[20] Bertin, E. (2012). *A concise introduction to the statistical physics of complex systems*. Springer.

[21] Bettenburg, N.; Hassan, A. E. (2010). Studying the Impact of Social Structures on Software Quality. *2010 IEEE 18th International Conference on Program Comprehension* , 124–133.

[22] Bettenburg, N.; Hassan, A. E.; Adams, B.; German, D. M. (2013). Management of community contributions. *Empirical Software Engineering* , 1–38.

[23] Bettenburg, N.; Just, S.; Schröter, A.; Weiss, C.; Premraj, R.; Zimmermann, T. (2008). What makes a good bug report? *Proceedings of the 16th ACM SIGSOFT/FSE International Symposium on Foundations of software engineering* , 308.

[24] Bettenburg, N.; Premraj, R.; Zimmermann, T. (2008). Duplicate bug reports considered harmful really? In: *2008 IEEE International Conference on Software Maintenance*. Ieee, pp. 337–345.

[25] Bhattacharya, P.; Iliofotou, M.; Neamtiu, I.; Faloutsos, M. (2012). Graph-based analysis and prediction for software evolution. In: *proceedings of the 34th ICSE*. pp. 419–429.

[26] Bhattacharya, P.; Neamtiu, I. (2010). Fine-grained incremental learning and multi-feature tossing graphs to improve bug triaging. In: *IEEE International Conference on Software Maintenance*. Ieee, pp. 1–10.

[27] Bird, C.; Nagappan, N.; Gall, H.; Murphy, B.; Devanbu, P. (2009). Putting it all together: Using socio-technical networks to predict failures. In: *Software Reliability Engineering, 2009. ISSRE'09. 20th International Symposium on*. IEEE, pp. 109–119.

[28] Blincoe, K.; Valetto, G.; Goggins, S. (2012). Leveraging task contexts for managing developers' coordination. In: *ACM Conference on Computer Supported Cooperative Work*. pp. 1351–1360.

[29] Blincoe, K.; Valetto, G.; Goggins, S. (2012). Proximity: a measure to quantify the need for developers' coordination. In: *Proceedings of the ACM 2012 conference on Computer Supported Cooperative Work*. ACM, pp. 1351–1360.

[30] Blondel, V. D.; Guillaume, J.-L.; Lambiotte, R.; Lefebvre, E. (2008). Fast unfolding of communities in large networks. *Journal of Statistical Mechanics: Theory and Experiment* **2008(10)**, P10008.

[31] Bollen, J.; Mao, H.; Zeng, X.-j. (2011). Twitter mood predicts the stock market. *Journal of Computational Science* **2**, 1–8.

[32] Bradbury, D. (2013). The problem with Bitcoin. *Computer Fraud & Security* **2013(11)**, 5–8.

[33] Brown, N.; Cai, Y.; Guo, Y.; Kazman, R.; Kim, M.; Kruchten, P.; Lim, E.; MacCormack, A.; Nord, R.; Ozkaya, I.; *et al.* (2010). Managing technical debt in software-reliant systems. In: *Proceedings of the FSE/SDP workshop on Future of software engineering research*. ACM, pp. 47–52.

[34] Bryton, S.; Abreu, F. B. e. (2008). Modularity-oriented refactoring. In: *Software Maintenance and Reengineering, 2008. CSMR 2008. 12th European Conference on*. IEEE, pp. 294–297.

[35] Cantillon, D.; Davidson II, W. S.; Schweitzer, J. H. (2003). Measuring community social organization: Sense of community as a mediator in social disorganization theory. *Journal of Criminal Justice* **31(4)**, 321–339.

[36] Cataldo, M.; Herbsleb, J. D.; Carley, K. M. (2008). Socio-technical congruence: a framework for assessing the impact of technical and work dependencies on software development productivity. In: *Proceedings of the Second ACM-IEEE international symposium on Empirical software engineering and measurement*. ACM, pp. 2–11.

[37] Cataldo, M.; Mockus, A.; Roberts, J. A.; Herbsleb, J. D. (2009). Software dependencies, work dependencies, and their impact on failures. *Software Engineering, IEEE Transactions on* **35(6)**, 864–878.

[38] Chandra, J.; Scholtes, I.; Ganguly, N.; Schweitzer, F. (2012). A Tunable Mechanism for Identifying Trusted Nodes in Large Scale Distributed Networks. In: *Trust, Security and Privacy in Computing and Communications (TrustCom), 2012 IEEE 11th International Conference on*. IEEE, pp. 722–729.

[39] Charette, R. N. (2005). Why software fails. *IEEE spectrum* **42(9)**, 36.

[40] Chen, C.-T. (1998). *Linear system theory and design*. Oxford University Press, Inc.

[41] Chmiel, A.; Sienkiewicz, J.; Thelwall, M.; Paltoglou, G.; Buckley, K.; Kappas, A.; Hołyst, J. A. (2011). Collective Emotions Online and Their Influence on Community Life. *PLoS ONE* **6(7)**, e22207.

[42] Christakis, N. A.; Fowler, J. H. (2007). The spread of obesity in a large social network over 32 years. *New England journal of medicine* **357(4)**, 370–379.

[43] Conaldi, G.; Lomi, A.; Tonellato, M. (2012). Dynamic models of affiliation and the network structure of problem solving in an open source software project. *Organizational Research Methods* **15(3)**, 385–412.

[44] Crowston, K.; Howison, J. (2005). The social structure of Free and Open Source Software development. *First Monday* **10**.

[45] Crowston, K.; Howison, J.; Annabi, H. (2006). Information systems success in free and open source software development: Theory and measures. *Software Process: Improvement and Practice* **11(2)**, 123–148.

[46] Crowston, K.; Scozzi, B. (2004). Coordination practices within FLOSS development teams: The bug fixing process. *Computer Supported Acitivity Coordination* .

[47] Crowston, K.; Wei, K. (2006). Core and periphery in Free/Libre and Open Source software team communications. *System Sciences, 2006.* **00(C)**, 1–7.

[48] Crowston, K.; Wei, K.; Howison, J.; Wiggins, A. (2012). Free/Libre open-source software development: What we know and what we do not know. *ACM Computing Surveys* **44(2)**, 1–35.

[49] Cruz, J.; Dorea, C. (1998). Simple conditions for the convergence of simulated annealing type algorithms. *Journal of applied probability* , 885–892.

[50] Csardi, G.; Nepusz, T. (2006). The igraph software package for complex network research. *InterJournal* **Complex Systems**, 1695.

[51] Cubranic, D.; Murphy, G. C. (2004). Automatic bug triage using text categorization. In: *Proceedings of the Sixteenth International Conference on Software Engineering & Knowledge Engineering (SEKE'2004)*. pp. 92–97.

[52] Cunningham, W. (1992). The WyCash portfolio management system. In: *ACM SIGPLAN OOPS Messenger*. ACM, vol. 4, pp. 29–30.

[53] Cvijikj, I. P.; Michahelles, F. (2011). Monitoring Trends on Facebook. *2011 IEEE Ninth International Conference on Dependable, Autonomic and Secure Computing* , 895–902.

[54] Dallard, P.; Fitzpatrick, T.; Flint, A.; Low, A.; Smith, R. R.; Willford, M.; Roche, M. (2001). London Millennium Bridge: pedestrian-induced lateral vibration. *Journal of Bridge Engineering* **6(6)**, 412–417.

[55] D'Ambros, M.; Lanza, M.; Robbes, R. (2010). An extensive comparison of bug prediction approaches. In: *Mining Software Repositories (MSR), 2010 7th IEEE Working Conference on*. IEEE, pp. 31–41.

[56] Davis, J. S. (1990). Effect of modularity on maintainability of rule-based systems. *International Journal of Man-Machine Studies* **32(4)**, 439–447.

[57] Demeyer, S.; Ducasse, S.; Nierstrasz, O. (2000). Finding refactorings via change metrics. *ACM SIGPLAN Notices* **35(10)**, 166–177.

[58] Deng, S.; Mitsubuchi, T.; Shioda, K.; Shimada, T.; Sakurai, A. (2011). Combining Technical Analysis with Sentiment Analysis for Stock Price Prediction. *2011 IEEE Ninth International Conference on Dependable, Autonomic and Secure Computing* , 800–807.

[59] Di Lucca, G. A.; Di Penta, M.; Gradara, S. (2002). An approach to classify software maintenance requests. In: *Software Maintenance, 2002. Proceedings. International Conference on*. IEEE, pp. 93–102.

[60] Dijkstra, E. W. (1972). The humble programmer. *Communications of the ACM* **15(10)**, 859–866.

[61] Dijkstra, E. W. (1982). On the role of scientific thought. In: *Selected Writings on Computing: A Personal Perspective*, Springer. pp. 60–66.

[62] Doval, D.; Mancoridis, S.; Mitchell, B. S. (1999). Automatic clustering of software systems using a genetic algorithm. In: *Software Technology and Engineering Practice, 1999. STEP'99. Proceedings*. IEEE, pp. 73–81.

[63] Dror, G.; Pelleg, D.; Rokhlenko, O.; Szpektor, I. (2012). Churn prediction in new users of Yahoo! answers. In: *Proceedings of the 21st international conference companion on World Wide Web - WWW '12 Companion*. New York, New York, USA, p. 829.

[64] Du Bois, B.; Demeyer, S.; Verelst, J. (2004). Refactoring-improving coupling and cohesion of existing code. In: *Reverse Engineering, 2004. Proceedings. 11th Working Conference on*. IEEE, pp. 144–151.

[65] Ehrlich, K.; Cataldo, M. (2012). All-for-one and one-for-all?: a multi-level analysis of communication patterns and individual performance in geographically distributed software development. In: *Proceedings of the ACM 2012 conference on Computer Supported Cooperative Work*. CSCW '12, New York, NY, USA: ACM, pp. 945–954.

[66] Ehrlich, K.; Valetto, G.; Helander, M. (2007). Seeing inside: Using social network analysis to understand patterns of collaboration and coordination in global software teams. In: *ICGSE*. IEEE, pp. 297–298.

[67] Ellis, G. F. (2005). Physics and the real world. *Physics Today* **58(7)**, 49.

[68] Ellis, G. F. (2005). Physics, complexity and causality. *Nature* **435(7043)**, 743–743.

[69] Evans, P.; Wolf, B. (2005). Collaboration rules. *Harvard Bus. Rev.* **7**, 96–103.

[70] Fershtman, C.; Gandal, N. (2011). Direct and indirect knowledge spillovers: the "social network" of open-source projects. *The RAND Journal of Economics* **42(1)**, 70–91.

[71] Fershtman, C.; Gandal, N. (2011). Direct and indirect knowledge spillovers: the "social network" of open-source projects. *The RAND Journal of Economics* **42(1)**, 70–91.

[72] Filman, R.; Elrad, T.; Clarke, S.; *et al.* (2004). *Aspect-oriented software development.* Addison-Wesley Professional.

[73] Fortuna, M.; Bonachela, J.; Levin, S. (2011). Evolution of a modular software network. *Proceedings of the National Academy of Sciences* **108**, 19985–19989.

[74] Fowler, M. (1999). *Refactoring: improving the design of existing code.* Addison-Wesley Professional.

[75] Freeman, L. C. (1979). Centrality in social networks conceptual clarification. *Social networks* **1(3)**, 215–239.

[76] Gacek, C.; Arief, B. (2004). The Many Meanings of Open Source. *IEEE Software* **21**, 34–40.

[77] Gall, H.; Hajek, K.; Jazayeri, M. (1998). Detection of logical coupling based on product release history. In: *Software Maintenance, 1998. Proceedings. International Conference on.* IEEE, pp. 190–198.

[78] Garas, A.; Garcia, D.; Skowron, M.; Schweitzer, F. (2012). Emotional persistence in online chatting communities. *Scientific Reports* **2**, 402.

[79] Garas, A.; Schweitzer, F.; Havlin, S. (2012). A k-shell decomposition method for weighted networks. *New Journal of Physics* **14(8)**, 083030.

[80] Garcia, D.; Garas, A.; Schweitzer, F. (2012). Positive words carry less information than negative words. *EPJ Data Science* **1(1)**, 3.

[81] Garcia, D.; Mavrodiev, P.; Schweitzer, F. (2013). Social Resilience in Online Communities: The Autopsy of Friendster. *arXiv preprint arXiv:1302.6109* .

[82] Garcia, D.; Mendez, F.; Serdült, U.; Schweitzer, F. (2012). Political polarization and popularity in online participatory media. In: *Proceedings of the workshop on Politics, elections and data.* pp. 3–10.

[83] Garcia, D.; Schweitzer, F. (2011). Emotions in Product Reviews – Empirics and Models. *Proceedings of 2011 IEEE International Conference on Social Computing, SocialCom* , 483–488.

[84] Garcia, D.; Schweitzer, F. (2012). Modeling online collective emotions. In: *Proceedings of the 2012 workshop on Data-driven user behavioral modelling and mining from social media - DUBMMSM '12*. p. 37.

[85] Geipel, M. M. (2012). Modularity, Dependence And Change. *Advances in Complex Systems* **15(06)**.

[86] Geipel, M. M.; Schweitzer, F. (2012). The Link between Dependency and Co-Change: Empirical Evidence. *IEEE Transactions on Software Engineering* **38(6)**, 1432–1444.

[87] Ghezzi, C.; Jazayeri, M.; Mandrioli, D. (2003). *Fundamentals of Software Engineering*. Prentice Hall, 2nd edn.

[88] Giuri, P.; Rullani, F.; Torrisi, S. (2008). Explaining leadership in virtual teams: the case of open source software. *Inform. Econ. Policy* **20**, 305–315.

[89] Gladwell, M. (1993). The tipping point. *How Little Things Can Make a Big Differ* .

[90] Glass, R. L. (2002). *Facts and fallacies of software engineering*. Addison-Wesley Professional.

[91] Goldenfeld, N.; Kadanoff, L. P. (1999). Simple lessons from complexity. *Science* **284(5411)**, 87–89.

[92] Goleman, D. (2003). What makes a leader. *Organizational Influence Processes (Porter, LW, et al. Eds.), New York, ME Sharpe* , 229–241.

[93] González-Bailón, S.; Borge-Holthoefer, J.; Rivero, A.; Moreno, Y. (2011). The dynamics of protest recruitment through an online network. *Scientific reports* **1**, 197.

[94] Granville, V.; Krivánek, M.; Rasson, J.-P. (1994). Simulated annealing: A proof of convergence. *Pattern Analysis and Machine Intelligence, IEEE Transactions on* **16(6)**, 652–656.

[95] Grewal, R.; Lilien, G.; Mallapragada, G. (2006). Location, location, location: How network embeddedness affects project success in open source systems. *Management Science* **52(7)**, 1043.

[96] Guo, P.; Zimmermann, T. (2010). Characterizing and predicting which bugs get fixed: An empirical study of Microsoft Windows. In: *Proceedings of the 32nd ACM/IEEE Conference on Software Engineering*. pp. 495–504.

[97] Haldane, A. G.; May, R. M. (2011). Systemic risk in banking ecosystems. *Nature* **469(7330)**, 351–355.

[98] Hall, J. F. (1961). *Psychology of motivation*. Lippincott.

[99] Hall, R.; Pauls, K.; McCulloch, S.; Savage, D. (2011). *OSGi in action: Creating modular applications in Java*. Manning Publications Co.

[100] Hardin, G. (1968). The Tragedy of the Commons. *Science* **162(5364)**, 1243–8.

[101] Hashmi, S. I.; Clerc, V.; Razavian, M.; Manteli, C.; Tamburri, D. A.; Lago, P.; Nitto, E. D.; Richardson, I. (2011). Using the cloud to facilitate global software development challenges. In: *Global Software Engineering Workshop (ICGSEW), 2011 Sixth IEEE International Conference on*. IEEE, pp. 70–77.

[102] Hastie, T.; Tibshirani, R.; Friedman, J.; Franklin, J. (2005). The elements of statistical learning: data mining, inference and prediction. *The Mathematical Intelligencer* **27(2)**, 83–85.

[103] Hautus, E. (2002). Improving Java software through package structure analysis. In: *The 6th IASTED International Conference Software Engineering and Applications*.

[104] He, P.; Li, B.; Huang, Y. (2012). Applying Centrality Measures to the Behavior Analysis of Developers in Open Source Software Community. *Second IEEE International Conference on Cloud and Green Computing*, 418–423.

[105] Helbing, D. (2001). Traffic and related self-driven many-particle systems. *Reviews of modern physics* **73(4)**, 1067.

[106] Herbsleb, J. D. (2007). Global software engineering: The future of socio-technical coordination. In: *2007 Future of Software Engineering*. IEEE Computer Society, pp. 188–198.

[107] Herrera, O.; Znati, T. (2007). Modeling Churn in P2P Networks. In: *40th IEEE Annual Simulation Symposium (ANSS'07)*. pp. 33–40.

[108] Hill, L. A. (1998). Developing the star performer. *Leader to Leader* **1998(8)**, 30–37.

[109] Hollander, M.; Wolfe, D. (1999). *Nonparametric statistical methods*. Wiley-Interscience.

[110] Hooimeijer, P.; Weimer, W. (2007). Modeling bug report quality. In: *Proceedings of the 22nd IEEE/ACM international conference on Automated software engineering*. pp. 34–43.

[111] Horwitz, S.; Reps, T. (1992). The use of program dependence graphs in software engineering. In: *ICSE Proceedings*. ACM, pp. 392–411.

[112] Howison, J.; Inoue, K.; Crowston, K. (2006). Social dynamics of free and open source team communications. *Open Source Systems* , 319–330.

[113] Hromkovic, J. (2011). *Theoretical Computer Science: Introduction to Automata, Computability, Complexity, Algorithmics, Randomization, Communication, and Cryptography*. Springer.

[114] Hu, Y. (2005). Efficient, high-quality force-directed graph drawing. *Mathematica Journal* **10(1)**, 37–71.

[115] Jansen, S.; Finkelstein, A.; Brinkkemper, S. (2009). A sense of community: A research agenda for software ecosystems. In: *Software Engineering-Companion Volume, 2009. ICSE-Companion 2009. 31st International Conference on*. IEEE, pp. 187–190.

[116] Jensen, C.; King, S.; Kuechler, V. (2011). Joining Free/Open source software communities: An analysis of newbies' first interactions on project mailing lists. In: *System Sciences (HICSS), 2011 44th Hawaii International Conference on*. IEEE, pp. 1–10.

[117] Johnson, N. (2009). *Simply Complexity: A clear guide to complexity theory*. Oneworld Publications.

[118] Johnson, S. (2012). *Emergence: The connected lives of ants, brains, cities, and software*. Simon and Schuster.

[119] Kappas, A. (2013). Social regulation of emotion: messy layers. *Frontiers in psychology* **4(February)**, 51.

[120] Karnstedt, M.; Hennessy, T.; Chan, J.; Hayes, C. (2010). Churn in Social Networks: A Discussion Boards Case Study. In: *2010 IEEE Second International Conference on Social Computing*. pp. 233–240.

[121] Kawale, J.; Pal, A.; Srivastava, J. (2009). Churn Prediction in MMORPGs: A Social Influence Based Approach. In: *IEEE International Conference on Computational Science and Engineering*. pp. 423–428.

[122] Kirkpatrick, S.; Jr., D. G.; Vecchi, M. P. (1983). Optimization by simmulated annealing. *science* **220(4598)**, 671–680.

[123] Knoke, D.; Yang, S. (2008). *Social network analysis*, vol. 154. Sage.

[124] Kohring, G. A. (2009). Complex Dependencies in Large Software Systems. *Advances in Complex Systems* **12(6)**, 565–581.

[125] Koschke, R. (2002). Atomic architectural component recovery for program understanding and evolution. In: *Software Maintenance, 2002. Proceedings. International Conference on*. IEEE, pp. 478–481.

[126] von Krogh, G.; von Hippel, E. (2006). The promise of research on open source software. *Management Science* **52(7)**, 975.

[127] Kucuktunc, O.; Cambazoglu, B. B.; Weber, I.; Ferhatosmanoglu, H. (2012). A large-scale sentiment analysis for Yahoo! answers. In: *Proceedings of the fifth ACM international conference on Web search and data mining - WSDM '12*. New York, New York, USA, p. 633.

[128] Kwan, I.; Schroter, A.; Damian, D. (2011). Does socio-technical congruence have an effect on software build success? a study of coordination in a software project. *Software Engineering, IEEE Transactions on* **37(3)**, 307–324.

[129] Lanubile, F.; Ebert, C.; Prikladnicki, R.; Vizcaíno, A. (2010). Collaboration tools for global software engineering. *Software, IEEE* **27(2)**, 52–55.

[130] Leiserson, C. E.; Rivest, R. L.; Stein, C.; Cormen, T. H. (2001). *Introduction to algorithms*. The MIT press.

[131] Lerner, J.; Tirole, J. (2002). Some simple economics of open source. *Journal of Industrial Economics* , 197–234.

[132] Levesque, L. L.; Wilson, J. M.; Wholey, D. R. (2001). Cognitive divergence and shared mental models in software development project teams. *Journal of Organizational Behavior* **22(2)**, 135–144.

[133] Li, W.; Henry, S. (1993). Object-oriented metrics that predict maintainability. *Journal of systems and software* **23(2)**, 111–122.

[134] Maguire, B.; Hagan, P. (2007). Disasters and communities: understanding social resilience. *Australian Journal of Emergency Management, The* **22(2)**, 16.

[135] Mahdavi, K.; Harman, M.; Hierons, R. M. (2003). A multiple hill climbing approach to software module clustering. In: *Software Maintenance, 2003. ICSM 2003. Proceedings. International Conference on*. IEEE, pp. 315–324.

[136] Manteli, C.; Vliet, H. v.; Hooff, B. v. d. (2012). Adopting a Social Network Perspective in Global Software Development. In: *Global Software Engineering (ICGSE), 2012 IEEE Seventh International Conference on*. IEEE, pp. 124–133.

[137] Mazzocchi, F. (2012). Complexity and the reductionism–holism debate in systems biology. *Wiley Interdisciplinary Reviews: Systems Biology and Medicine* **4(5)**, 413–427.

[138] McMillan, D. W.; Chavis, D. M. (1986). Sense of community: A definition and theory. *Journal of community psychology* **14(1)**, 6–23.

[139] Messerschmitt, D. G.; Szyperski, C. (2005). Software ecosystem: understanding an indispensable technology and industry. *MIT Press Books* **1**.

[140] Metropolis, N.; Rosenbluth, A. W.; Rosenbluth, M. N.; Teller, A. H.; Teller, E. (1953). Equation of state calculations by fast computing machines. *The journal of chemical physics* **21**, 1087.

[141] Mèuller-Scholer, C.; Schmeck, H.; Ungerer, T. (2011). *Organic computing–a paradigm shift for complex systems*, vol. 1. Springer.

[142] Michalski, R.; Jankowski, J.; Kazienko, P. (2012). Negative Effects of Incentivised Viral Campaigns for Activity in Social Networks. *2012 IEEE Second International Conference on Cloud and Green Computing* , 391–398.

[143] Migdał, P. (2012). Tag Graph Map of StackExchange. GitHub repository, `https://github.com/stared/tag-graph-map-of-stackexchange`.

[144] Mika, P.; Greaves, M. (2012). Editorial: Semantic Web & Web 2.0. *Web Semantics: Science, Services and Agents on the World Wide Web* **6(1)**.

[145] Mitchell, M. (2009). *Complexity: a guided tour*. Oxford University Press.

[146] Mitra, D.; Romeo, F.; Sangiovanni-Vincentelli, A. (1985). Convergence and finite-time behavior of simulated annealing. In: *Decision and Control, 1985 24th IEEE Conference on*. IEEE, vol. 24, pp. 761–767.

[147] Mockus, A.; Fielding, R. T.; Herbsleb, J. D. (2002). Two case studies of open source software development: Apache and Mozilla. *ACM Transactions on Software Engineering and Methodology* **11(3)**, 309–346.

[148] Monasor, M. J.; Vizcaino, A.; Piattini, M.; Noll, J.; Beecham, S. (2013). Towards a Global Software Development Community Web: Identifying Patterns and Scenarios. In: *Global Software Engineering Workshops (ICGSEW), 2013 IEEE 8th International Conference on*. IEEE, pp. 41–46.

[149] Myers, C. R. (2003). Software systems as complex networks: Structure, function, and evolvability of software collaboration graphs. *Physical Review E* **68(4)**, 046116.

[150] Newman, M. E. J. (2003). Mixing Patterns in Networks. *Phy. Review E* **67**, 026126.

[151] Newman, M. E. J. (2003). The structure and function of complex networks. *SIAM review*, 167–256.

[152] Newman, M. E. J. (2010). *Networks: an introduction*. Oxford Univ Press.

[153] Newman, M. E. J.; Girvan, M. (2004). Finding and evaluating community structure in networks. *Physical Review E* **69**, 026113.

[154] Nia, R.; Bird, C.; Devanbu, P.; Filkov, V. (2010). Validity of network analyses in Open Source Projects. In: *proceedings of the 7th IEEE Working Conference on Mining Software Repositories (MSR)*. IEEE, pp. 201–209.

[155] Onyx, J.; Bullen, P. (2000). Measuring social capital in five communities. *The Journal of Applied Behavioral Science* **36(1)**, 23–42.

[156] O'Regan, G. (2012). *A brief history of computing*. Springer, 2nd edn.

[157] Palla, G.; Barabási, A.-L.; Vicsek, T. (2007). Quantifying social group evolution. *Nature* **446(7136)**, 664–667.

[158] Paltoglou, G.; Gobron, S.; Skowron, M.; Thelwall, M.; Thalmann, D. (2010). Sentiment analysis of informal textual communication in cyberspace. In: *In Proc. Engage 2010*. pp. 13–25.

[159] Parnas, D. L. (1972). On the criteria to be used in decomposing systems into modules. *Communications of the ACM* **15(12)**, 1053–1058.

[160] Parnas, D. L.; Clements, P. C.; Weiss, D. M. (1985). The modular structure of complex systems. *Software Engineering, IEEE Transactions on* **11(3)**, 259–266.

[161] Parsa, S.; Bushehrian, O. (2007). Genetic clustering with constraints. *Journal of research and practice in information technology* **39(1)**, 47–60.

[162] Pfitzner, R.; Garas, A. (2012). Emotional divergence influences information spreading in Twitter. In: *AAAI ICWSM 2012*. pp. 2–5.

[163] Pfitzner, R.; Garas, A.; Schweitzer, F. (2012). Emotional Divergence Influences Information Spreading in Twitter. In: *ICWSM*.

[164] Pfitzner, R.; Scholtes, I.; Garas, A.; Tessone, C. J.; Schweitzer, F. (2013). Betweenness preference: quantifying correlations in the topological dynamics of temporal networks. *Physical review letters* **110(19)**, 198701.

[165] Pironio, S.; Aharonov, D. (2013). Quantum physics: A grip on misbehaviour. *Nature* **496(7446)**, 436–437.

[166] Podgurski, A.; Leon, D.; Francis, P. (2003). Automated support for classifying software failure reports. In: *Proceedings of the 25th International Conference on Software Engineering, ICSE'03*. pp. 465–475.

[167] Poshyvanyk, D.; Marcus, A. (2006). The conceptual coupling metrics for object-oriented systems. In: *Software Maintenance, 2006. ICSM'06. 22nd IEEE International Conference on*. IEEE, pp. 469–478.

[168] R Core Team (2012). *R: A Language and Environment for Statistical Computing*. R Foundation for Statistical Computing.

[169] Raccoon, L. (1995). The chaos model and the chaos cycle. *ACM SIGSOFT Software Engineering Notes* **20(1)**, 55–66.

[170] Raymond, E. S. (1999). The cathedral and the bazaar. *Knowledge, Technology & Policy* **12(3)**, 23–49.

[171] Rickles, D.; Hawe, P.; Shiell, A. (2007). A simple guide to chaos and complexity. *Journal of Epidemiology and Community Health* **61(11)**, 933–937.

[172] Robillard, P. N. (1999). The role of knowledge in software development. *Communications of the ACM* **42(1)**, 87–92.

[173] Robles, G.; Gonzalez-Barahona, J. (2006). Contributor Turnover in Libre Software Projects. In: E. Damiani; et al (eds.), *Open Source Systems*, Springer Boston, vol. 203. pp. 273–286.

[174] Rook, P. (1986). Controlling software projects. *Software Engineering Journal* **1(1)**, 7.

[175] Rovai, A. P. (2002). Building sense of community at a distance. *The International Review of Research in Open and Distance Learning* **3(1)**.

[176] Runeson, P.; Alexandersson, M.; Nyholm, O. (2007). Detection of Duplicate Defect Reports Using Natural Language Processing. *29th International Conference on Software Engineering (ICSE'07)* , 499–510.

[177] Sadowski, B.; Sadowski-Rasters, G.; Duysters, G. (2008). Transition of governance in a mature open software source community: evidence from the Debian case. *Inf. Econ. Policy* **20**, 323–332.

[178] Salton, G.; McGill, M. (1986). *Introduction to modern information retrieval*. McGraw-Hill, Inc.

[179] Sampson, R. J. (1991). Linking the micro-and macrolevel dimensions of community social organization. *Social Forces* **70(1)**, 43–64.

[180] Sarason, S. B. (1974). *The psychological sense of community: Prospects for a community psychology*. Jossey-Bass.

[181] Scacchi, W. (1984). Managing Software Engineering Projects: A Social Analysis. *Software Engineering, IEEE Transactions on* **SE-10(1)**, 49–59.

[182] Scholtes, I.; Tessone, C. J. (2012). Organic design of massively distributed systems: a complex networks perspective. *Informatik-Spektrum* **35(2)**, 75–86.

[183] Scholtes, I.; Wider, N.; Pfitzner, R.; Garas, A.; Tessone, C. J.; Schweitzer, F. (2013). Slow-Down vs. Speed-Up of Information Diffusion in Non-Markovian Temporal Networks. *arXiv preprint arXiv:1307.4030* .

[184] Schweitzer, F. (2007). *Brownian agents and active particles: collective dynamics in the natural and social sciences*. Springer.

[185] Schweitzer, F.; Fagiolo, G.; Sornette, D.; Vega-Redondo, F.; Vespignani, A.; White, D. R. (2009). Economic networks: The new challenges. *science* **325(5939)**, 422.

[186] Schweitzer, F.; Garcia, D. (2010). An agent-based model of collective emotions in online communities. *The European Physical Journal B* **77(4)**, 533–545.

[187] Scott, A. (2004). Reductionism revisited. *Journal of Consciousness Studies* **11(2)**, 51–68.

[188] Scott, J. (1988). Social network analysis. *Sociology* **22(1)**, 109–127.

[189] Scozzi, B.; Crowston, K.; Yeliz Eseryel, U.; Li, Q. (2008). Shared mental models among open source software developers. In: *Hawaii International Conference on System Sciences, Proceedings of the 41st Annual.* IEEE, pp. 306–306.

[190] Seaman, C. B. (1999). Qualitative methods in empirical studies of software engineering. *Software Engineering, IEEE Transactions on* **25(4)**, 557–572.

[191] Serrano, N.; Ciordia, I. (2005). Bugzilla, ITracker, and other bug trackers. *Software, IEEE* **22(2)**, 11–13.

[192] Shardanand, U.; Maes, P. (1995). Social information filtering: algorithms for automating "word of mouth". In: *Proceedings of the SIGCHI conference on Human factors in computing systems.* ACM Press/Addison-Wesley Publishing Co., pp. 210–217.

[193] Shihab, E.; Ihara, A.; Kamei, Y.; Ibrahim, W. M.; Ohira, M.; Adams, B.; Hassan, A. E.; Matsumoto, K.-i. (2010). Predicting Re-opened Bugs: A Case Study on the Eclipse Project. In: *Proceedings of the 2010 17th IEEE Working Conference on Reverse Engineering.* pp. 249–258.

[194] Snijders, T. A.; Lomi, A.; Torló, V. J. (2013). A model for the multiplex dynamics of two-mode and one-mode networks, with an application to employment preference, friendship, and advice. *Social networks* **35(2)**, 265–276.

[195] Society, I. C. (1990). IEEE Standard Glossary of Software Engineering Terminology. *IEEE Std 610.12-1990* , 1–84.

[196] Somasundaram, K.; Murphy, G. C. (2012). Automatic categorization of bug reports using latent Dirichlet allocation. In: *Proceedings of the 5th India Software Engineering Conference.* ISEC '12, ACM, pp. 125–130.

[197] Steinfield, C.; DiMicco, J. M.; Ellison, N. B.; Lampe, C. (2009). Bowling online: social networking and social capital within the organization. In: *Proceedings of the fourth international conference on Communities and technologies.* ACM, pp. 245–254.

[198] Steinmacher, I.; Wiese, I.; Chaves, A.; Gerosa, M. (2013). Why do newcomers abandon open source software projects? In: *Cooperative and Human Aspects of Software Engineering (CHASE), 2013 6th International Workshop on.* pp. 25–32.

[199] Stevens, W. P.; Myers, G. J.; Constantine, L. L. (1974). Structured design. *IBM Systems Journal* **13(2)**, 115–139.

[200] Streeter, C. L.; Gillespie, D. F. (1993). Social network analysis. *Journal of Social Service Research* **16(1-2)**, 201–222.

[201] Strogatz, S. (2000). *Nonlinear dynamics and chaos: with applications to physics, biology, chemistry and engineering.* Perseus Books Group.

[202] Subelj, L.; Bajec, M. (2011). Community structure of complex software systems: Analysis and applications. *Physica A: Statistical Mechanics and its Applications* .

[203] Subramaniam, C.; Sen, R.; Nelson, M. (2009). Determinants of open source software project success: A longitudinal study. *Decision Support Systems* **46(2)**, 576–585.

[204] Tamburri, D. A.; Kruchten, P.; Lago, P.; van Vliet, H. (2013). What Is Social Debt in Software Engineering? In: *Proceedings of the CHASE '13 ICSE Workshop*.

[205] Tamburri, D. A.; Lago, P.; Vliet, H. V.; Nitto, E. d. (2012). On the Nature of GSE Organizational Social Structures: An Empirical Study. In: *Global Software Engineering (ICGSE), 2012 IEEE Seventh International Conference on*. IEEE, pp. 114–123.

[206] Tempero, E.; Anslow, C.; Dietrich, J.; Han, T.; Li, J.; Lumpe, M.; Melton, H.; Noble, J. (2010). Qualitas Corpus: A Curated Collection of Java Code for Empirical Studies. In: *2010 APSEC*. pp. 336–345.

[207] Tessier, J. (2012). The Dependency Finder User Manual. . Dependency Finder (2001-2012). Revised BSD License.

[208] Tessone, C. J.; Geipel, M. M.; Schweitzer, F. (2011). Sustainable growth in complex networks. *Europhysics Letters* **96**, 58005.

[209] Tessone, C. J.; Geipel, M. M.; Schweitzer, F. (2011). Sustainable growth in complex networks. *EPL (Europhysics Letters)* **96**, 58005.

[210] Thelwall, M.; Buckley, K.; Paltoglou, G. (2012). Sentiment strength detection for the social web. *Journal of the American Society for Information Science and Technology* **63(1)**, 163–173.

[211] Thelwall, M.; Buckley, K.; Paltoglou, G.; Skowron, M.; Garcia, D.; Gobron, S.; Ahn, J.; Kappas, A.; Kuster, D.; Janusz, A. (2013). Damping Sentiment Analysis in Online Communication : Discussions , Monologs and Dialogs. In: *Proceedings of the 25th International Conference on Computational Linguistics (COLING)*. pp. 1–12.

[212] Tononi, G.; Edelman, G. M. (1998). Consciousness and complexity. *science* **282(5395)**, 1846–1851.

[213] Trist, E. (1981). The evolution of socio-technical systems. *Occasional paper* **2**, 1981.

[214] Umeda, Y.; Fukushige, S.; Tonoike, K.; Kondoh, S. (2008). Product modularity for life cycle design. *CIRP Annals-Manufacturing Technology* **57(1)**, 13–16.

[215] Uzzi, B. (1996). The sources and consequences of embeddedness for the economic performance of organizations: The network effect. *American sociological review* , 674–698.

[216] Valetto, G.; Chulani, S.; Williams, C. (2008). Balancing the value and risk of sociotechnical congruence. In: *Workshop on Sociotechnical Congruence*.

[217] Valetto, G.; Helander, M.; Ehrlich, K.; Chulani, S.; Wegman, M.; Williams, C. (2007). Using software repositories to investigate socio-technical congruence in development projects. In: *MSR '07*. IEEE, pp. 25–25.

[218] Van Regenmortel, M. H. (2004). Reductionism and complexity in molecular biology. *EMBO reports* **5(11)**, 1016.

[219] Walter, F. E.; Battiston, S.; Schweitzer, F. (2009). Personalised and dynamic trust in social networks. In: *Proceedings of the third ACM conference on Recommender systems - RecSys '09*. pp. 197–204.

[220] Wang, J.; Carroll, J. M. (2011). Beyond fixing bugs: case studies of creative collaboration in open source software bug fixing processes. In: *Proceedings of the 8th ACM conference on Creativity and cognition*. pp. 397–398.

[221] Wang, X.; Zhang, L.; Xie, T.; Anvik, J.; Sun, J. (2008). An approach to detecting duplicate bug reports using natural language and execution information. *Proceedings of the 13th international conference on Software engineering - ICSE '08* , 461.

[222] Wasserman, S.; Faust, K. (1994). *Social Network Analysis: Methods and Applications*. Cambridge University Press.

[223] Weber, S. (2004). *The success of open source*, vol. 368. Cambridge Univ Press.

[224] West, D. B. (2001). *Introduction to graph theory*. Prentice hall Englewood Cliffs, second edn.

[225] West, D. B. (2001). *Introduction to Graph Theory*. Prentice Hall, second edn.

[226] West, J.; O'Mahony, S. (2005). Contrasting community building in sponsored and community founded open source projects. In: *System Sciences, 2005. HICSS'05. Proceedings of the 38th Annual Hawaii International Conference on.* IEEE, pp. 196c–196c.

[227] Whitesides, G. M.; Ismagilov, R. F. (1999). Complexity in chemistry. *science* **284(5411)**, 89–92.

[228] Whitworth, B. (2006). Socio-technical systems. *Encyclopedia of human computer interaction*, 533–541.

[229] Wolf, T.; Schroter, A. (2009). Predicting build failures using social network analysis on developer communication. In: *Proceedings of the 31st.* pp. 1–11.

[230] Wolf, T.; Schroter, A.; Damian, D. (2009). Mining task-based social networks to explore collaboration in software teams. *IEEE Software*, 58–66.

[231] Wu, F. Y. (1982). The Potts model. *Reviews of Modern Physics* **54**, 235.

[232] Wu, J.; Hassan, A. E.; Holt, R. C. (2005). Comparison of clustering algorithms in the context of software evolution. In: *Software Maintenance, 2005. ICSM'05. Proceedings of the 21st IEEE International Conference on.* IEEE, pp. 525–535.

[233] Wu, S.; Das Sarma, A.; Fabrikant, A.; Lattanzi, S.; Tomkins, A. (2013). Arrival and departure dynamics in social networks. In: *Proceedings of the sixth ACM international conference on Web search and data mining - WSDM '13.* New York, New York, USA, p. 233.

[234] Wu, Y.; Wong, J.; Deng, Y.; Chang, K. (2011). An Exploration of Social Media in Public Opinion Convergence: Elaboration Likelihood and Semantic Networks on Political Events. *2011 IEEE Ninth International Conference on Dependable, Autonomic and Secure Computing*, 903–910.

[235] Wu, Y.; Zhou, C.; Xiao, J.; Kurths, J.; Schellnhuber, H. J. (2010). Evidence for a bimodal distribution in human communication. *Proceedings of the National Academy of Sciences of the United States of America* **107(44)**, 18803–8.

[236] Xuan, J.; Jiang, H.; Ren, Z.; Zou, W. (2012). Developer prioritization in bug repositories. In: *Proceedings of the 2012 International Conference on Software Engineering, ICSE.* pp. 25–35.

[237] Zanetti, M. S. (2012). The co-evolution of socio-technical structures in sustainable software development: Lessons from the open source software communities. In: *Proceedings of the 34th ICSE*. IEEE Press, pp. 1587–1590.

[238] Zanetti, M. S. (2013). *A complex systems approach to software engineering*. Ph.D. thesis, ETH Zürich.

[239] Zanetti, M. S.; Sarigol, E.; Scholtes, I.; Tessone, C. J.; Schweitzer, F. (2012). A quantitative study of social organisation in open source software communities. In: *Proceedings of the ICCSW '12 - Imperial College Computing Student Workshop*. Schloss Dagstuhl, vol. 28, pp. 116–122.

[240] Zanetti, M. S.; Scholtes, I.; Tessone, C. J.; Schweitzer, F. (2013). Categorizing bugs with social networks: A case study on four open source software communities. In: *Proceedings of the ICSE '13*. pp. 1032–1041.

[241] Zanetti, M. S.; Scholtes, I.; Tessone, C. J.; Schweitzer, F. (2013). The rise and fall of a central contributor: Dynamics of social organization and performance in the Gentoo community. In: *Proceedings of the CHASE '13 ICSE Workshop*. pp. 49–56.

[242] Zanetti, M. S.; Schweitzer, F. (2012). A network perspective on software modularity. In: *Architecture of Computing Systems (ARCS) Workshops 2012*. GI, IEEE, pp. 175–186.

[243] Zhang, L.; Jia, Y.; Zhou, B.; Han, Y. (2012). Microblogging Sentiment Analysis Using Emotional Vector. *2012 IEEE Second International Conference on Cloud and Green Computing*, 430–433.

[244] Zheleva, E.; Sharara, H.; Getoor, L. (2009). Co-evolution of social and affiliation networks. In: *Proceedings of the 15th ACM SIGKDD international conference on Knowledge discovery and data mining - KDD '09*. ACM Press, p. 1007.

[245] Zhou, M.; Mockus, A. (2012). What Make Long Term Contributors: Willingness and Opportunity in OSS Community. In: *Proceedings of the 34th ICSE*. pp. 518–528.

[246] Zimmermann, T.; Nagappan, N.; Guo, P. J.; Murphy, B. (2012). Characterizing and predicting which bugs get reopened. *2012 34th International Conference on Software Engineering (ICSE)*, 1074–1083.

# i want morebooks!

Buy your books fast and straightforward online - at one of world's fastest growing online book stores! Environmentally sound due to Print-on-Demand technologies.

## Buy your books online at
## www.get-morebooks.com

Kaufen Sie Ihre Bücher schnell und unkompliziert online – auf einer der am schnellsten wachsenden Buchhandelsplattformen weltweit! Dank Print-On-Demand umwelt- und ressourcenschonend produziert.

## Bücher schneller online kaufen
## www.morebooks.de

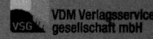

VDM Verlagsservicegesellschaft mbH
Heinrich-Böcking-Str. 6-8   Telefon: +49 681 3720 174   info@vdm-vsg.de
D - 66121 Saarbrücken      Telefax: +49 681 3720 1749  www.vdm-vsg.de

Printed by Books on Demand GmbH, Norderstedt / Germany